Diane Warner's

Complete Book of

Wedding Toasts

Revised Edition

Hundreds of Ways to Say "Congratulations!"

NEW PAGE BOOKS
A division of The Career Press, Inc.
Franklin Lakes, NJ

DIANE WARNER'S COMPLETE BOOK OF WEDDING TOASTS, REV. ED.
EDITED BY GINA TALUCCI
TYPESET BY EILEEN DOW MUNSON
Cover design by DesignConcept
Printed in the U.S.A. by Book-mart Press

To order this title, please call toll-free 1-800-CAREER-1 (NJ and
Canada: 201-848-0310) to order using VISA or MasterCard, or for
further information on books from Career Press.

The Career Press, Inc., 3 Tice Road, PO Box 687,
Franklin Lakes, NJ 07417
www.careerpress.com
www.newpagebooks.com

Library of Congress Cataloging-in-Publication Data
Warner, Diane
    Complete book of wedding toasts
    Diane Warner's complete book of wedding toasts : hundreds of
    ways to say "congratulations!" / Diane Warner.
        p.cm.
    Includes bibliographical references and index.
    ISBN 1-56414-815-7 (pbk.)
        1. Wedding toasts. I. Title: Complete book of wedding toasts. II.
        Title

PN6348.W4W37 2005
808.5'1—dc22

2005050483

With love to my grandson,

Jeffrey.

Acknowledgments

Many thanks to all of you, especially to the many members of wedding newsgroups on the Internet, who agreed to share your wedding toasts with my readers. I would also like to thank my sister, Linda Glass, who helped me with the research for this book, as did Linda Johnson, owner of Linda's Hallmark Shop in Turlock, California.

Finally, my thanks go to my editors, Betsy Sheldon, Ellen Scher, and Regina McAloney, for their help in putting this book together.

Also, my thanks go to Gina Talucci, Eileen Munson, Kristen Parkes, and Astrid deRidder for their help in putting this revised edition of the book together.

Contents

Introduction

The wedding toast—that poignantly tender gesture proposed to the newlyweds, a mysterious melding of poetry, quotations, prayer, wit, anecdote, and heart-rendered sentiment. Why so mysterious? Because the wedding toast has evolved through the years from a simple "To your health and happiness" to a soliloquy that requires personalization, preparation, practice, and presentation. It's enough to scare you half to death! In fact, statistics show that, next to dying, public speaking is most Americans' greatest fear, and the fear is understandable. After reading this book, however, your fears should be alleviated when you see how easy it really is to compose and deliver your toast.

You may wonder where the tradition of toasting began. Actually, it began under rather nefarious circumstances when the ancient Greeks initiated the art of toasting as a good faith gesture when the host took the first sip; thus assuring the guests that the punch wasn't spiked with poison, a common occurrence in those days. This is why the most familiar toast heard around the world has always been: "To your health."

The Romans later discovered that a small piece of charred bread, known as a piece of toast, mellowed the flavor of the wine being offered, which is how the term "toast" originated. And although wine was the Romans' toasting beverage of choice, once champagne was invented by the monk Dom Perignon in the 1600s, it became the preferred beverage served when toasting the bride. Champagne is still the most popular beverage served at weddings today, although it is perfectly proper to toast the couple with a nonalcoholic drink.

However, whether the toasting beverage contains alcohol or not, the important thing to remember is that a wedding toast is the one essential ingredient for any wedding reception. Although the reception may be an elaborate affair with a French-service sit-down dinner, dancing under the stars to your choice of orchestras, and a Fairmont cake presentation complete with spotlights and trumpet fanfare, without the wedding toast, it's just a very expensive party. The wedding toast is what sets it apart, which is why, if you plan to propose a toast during the reception, you must be prepared.

First, let's look at the etiquette of toasting:

Toasting etiquette

✧ Toasts are offered once all the guests have been served drinks, whether with a meal or, if no meal is served, with the wedding cake.

✧ The toasting beverage is poured in this order:

1. The bride.
2. The groom.

3. The maid or matron of honor.

4. All the other guests at the head table, with the
    best man being the last to receive his beverage.

✧ The best man usually offers the first toast, followed by the
    fathers, the groom, the bride, family friends, relatives, maid
    or matron of honor, the mothers, and anyone else who
    would like to.

✧ Wedding toasts are usually made to the bride or groom
    individually, the bride and groom as a couple, the brides-
    maids, the bride's parents, and the guests.

✧ If you're the one being toasted, stay seated and *never* raise
    your glass or drink from it during the toast itself. It is safe
    to take a sip, however, once everyone else has done so.

✧ Always stand when offering a toast.

Composing your toast

✧ A perfectly composed toast should be eloquent, poignant,
    whimsical, and witty.

✧ If you know you will be offering a toast during the wed-
    ding rehearsal or wedding reception, compose it ahead of
    time. When it comes time to offer your toast, you may use
    note cards to remind you of what you've decided to say
    or, if you're uncomfortable speaking in front of a group, it
    may be wise for you to commit your toast to memory.
    Never, however, *read* your toast because this will ruin its
    whimsical quality. By "whimsical," I mean that the toast
    should sound unrehearsed with an unpredictable quality
    about it, as if you just thought it up on the spot (even
    though you have been composing, editing, and practicing
    it for days!).

✧ Even though the wedding reception may be quite elegant and formal, and even though you may be considered an extremely literate and erudite person, avoid using pompous words or phrases. A toast is supposed to have a "warm and fuzzy" quality that springs from the heart and soul of the toaster.

✧ Avoid clichés. Instead, speak straight from your heart with as much sincerity and honest affection possible.

✧ Use personal anecdotes to spice up your toast. For example, tell about that Saturday afternoon when you and the groom were in third grade and you made a pact to "hate girls forever," or how the groom's only high school passions were sports and cars—girls were considered a silly waste of time and money, and so forth. If you can't think of any interesting or clever stories to include, or if you haven't known the bride or groom very long, do some research. Ask the bride's mother, for example, for any "inside information" she may be willing to reveal, or ask anyone else who has known the bride or groom over a length of time. Delve deeply and you're sure to uncover several fascinating tales that can be used in your toast.

✧ Bits of poetry, interesting quotations, and appropriate witticisms will enrich your toast, as well, show that you cared enough to give it some thought ahead of time.

✧ Avoid any jokes or anecdotes that are off-color or have ethnic or religious connotations.

✧ If you do decide to throw some humor into your toast, which is an excellent idea, be sure to end on a serious note.

✧ Steer clear of profanity. Foul or offensive language is considered taboo during any speech or toast.

✧ If it is the bride's or groom's second marriage, never mention either's first marriage during the toast.

✧ When composing your toast, never include any embarrassing references to the newlyweds' upcoming honeymoon, their future lovemaking, or any results thereof.

✧ Wedding toasts should be upbeat, so stay away from depressing subjects, such as a recent death in the family or anything else that would tend to bring tears to the eyes of the bride and groom. If there are to be tears, they should be from joyous hearts, not sad or grieving hearts.

✧ A wedding toast is usually between three and five minutes long. Any longer than that and you'll lose your audience!

Delivering your toast

✧ Stand to deliver your toast.

✧ Go easy on the alcoholic beverages before delivering your toast.

✧ Never rap a spoon against a cup or a glass to gain the guests' attention; instead, stand with the toasting glass held high until you have relative silence. Then, once you start to speak, everyone should quiet down to hear what you are saying. If there is a serious problem quieting things down, however, the master of ceremonies may ask for the guests' attention or the musicians may play a rousing fanfare as a prelude to the offering of the toasts.

✧ Use a microphone or speak loudly enough for all the guests to hear you. If you do decide to use a microphone, be sure to test it out *beforehand.* If you're the first speaker, you don't want to be the one who discovers the mike squeals when held too close to your mouth or that the volume is so low no one can hear you in the back of the room.

✧ Maintain eye contact with the bride and groom as you deliver the toast.

✧ Avoid negative body language, such as:

+ Chewing gum.

+ Hanging your head.

+ Shuffling from one foot to the other.

+ Jingling coins or keys in your pocket.

+ Holding your fingers in front of your mouth.

+ Placing one hand on the back of your neck.

+ Tugging at your collar or fiddling with your tie.

+ Tapping your foot.

+ Running your fingers through your hair.

+ Scratching yourself *anywhere*.

(Helpful hint: To avoid most of these annoying habits, hold the glass in one hand and a microphone in the other.)

✧ Avoid negative speech patterns as you deliver the toast, such as:

+ Repeating "You know," "Uhhh," or "I mean."

+ "Fast talk"—the tendency to talk faster as you progress through the toast. Not only will this distract from the content of your toast, but it will reveal your insecurity and give the impression: "I want to get this over with as soon as I can!" One quick cure for fast talk is to *breathe*. Toasters frequently forget to breathe, which rushes the toast, so concentrate on speaking in a leisurely way, *breathing* between each phrase.

✦ Letting your pitch rise. Not only is there a tendency to talk too fast, but to let your pitch spiral higher and higher, as well. Make a concerted effort to lower your voice to a richly modulated tone, raising your voice only as necessary to make a point, always returning to the lower pitch. But whatever you do, don't speak in a monotone.

(Helpful hint: To avoid all of these negative tendencies, practice delivering your toast to a "live audience," such as a trusted friend or family member. And as an added measure, have one of them record your toast on an audio- or videotape. Then, by seeing yourself as others see you and hearing yourself as others hear you, you'll be able to correct any little problems you may be having.)

✧ If you're absolutely terrified to speak in public, practice your toast in front of a full-length mirror every day before the wedding and try to remember this: Because a wedding is such a lighthearted, joyous occasion, you couldn't have a more undemanding audience. If you make a little mistake, or even if you end up reading your toast (which is the very worst thing that could happen), you will be forgiven! What will be remembered is the sentiment expressed, not some trifling faux pas.

✧ Smile!

This book contains the largest compilation of wedding toasts ever assembled, many gleaned from hundreds of one-on-one personal interviews as well as electronic interviews conducted over the Internet. Some of the most interesting and creative toasts were contributed by members of various wedding-related newsgroups on the Web. Although many of these toasts have been personalized to include stories about the newlyweds and their relationships to the toasters, they will serve to whet your creative juices as you ponder your own relationship to the bride or groom and experiences you may have had throughout the years.

As you read through this book, it may be a good idea for you to highlight your favorite phrases, quotations, or anecdotes as you go along, which can then be used or modified as you compose your own toast.

 Have fun!

Chapter 1

Traditional Toasts for the
Bride and Groom

The toasts included in this chapter are basic and simple, and may be exactly what you were hoping to find, although the trend today is toward more personalized wedding toasts. However, if you decide to adopt one of these traditional toasts as your own, deliver it in a dignified way with as much sincerity as possible.

Traditional toasts to the bride

Ladies and gentleman, please stand with me as we join in the traditional toast to the bride: health, happiness, and all the best life has to offer. To _____ .

It has been my pleasure to know _____ (the bride) all her life, and no one is more delighted than I to see her marry _____ (the groom). Ladies and gentlemen, please join with me in a toast to the bride: here's to your happiness, today and always.

_____ , there was never a bride more beautiful and radiant than you are today. Best wishes for a joyous married life, full of good health and happiness.

Traditional toasts to the bride and groom

Ladies and gentlemen, please stand with me as we raise our glasses in a toast to the bride and groom. _____ and _____ , we wish you a lifetime of health and happiness.

> A Finnish bride wears a golden crown during the ceremony and then during the reception that follows she is blindfolded and surrounded by all the unmarried women. Whoever the blindfolded bride crowns will be the next to marry.

I feel honored to have been asked to give the traditional toast to the bride and groom on this momentous occasion:

_____ and _____ , may your lives be filled with joy, good health, and a lifetime of happiness.

_____ and _____ , I toast you. May your joys be many and your troubles be few, with only success and good health following you.

To the happy couple: May your future be filled with wine and roses.

May all your days be as happy as the ones before.

_____ and _____ , I toast you.

> An Australian tribesman kept it very simple: He became "engaged" by shooting a barbless arrow through the leg of a maiden and then became "married" by removing the arrow after he carried her to his home.

Please stand and join me in this traditional toast to the bride and groom: May the most you ever wish for be the least you ever receive.

Ladies and gentlemen, it is now my pleasure to propose a toast to the happy couple: To love, which is nothing unless it's divided by two.

Here's to the husband—and here's to the wife; may they remain lovers for life.

It is thought to be good luck for a bride to sew a strand of her own hair into her wedding gown.

I toast you, _____ and _____ , as I wish you all the luck and happiness in this world. May God bless your marriage, and may you have a happy and contented home.

It is now my honor to toast the bride and groom. To _____ and _____ , two very nice people. I wish you good health, happiness, and a wonderful life together. Congratulations.

Join me in a toast to our newlyweds: May the happiest day of your past be the saddest day of your future.

20

At a Dutch wedding the bride's cake is often topped with a windmill and the groom's with a pair of wooden shoes; girls dressed in Dutch costume distribute tulip and crocus bulbs to the guests.

Please join me as we propose a toast to the happy couple: Our good wishes go with you for happiness and a long and prosperous life.

May all your troubles be little ones; may all your troubles be small; may all your troubles be light as air; may you have no troubles at all.

I would like to propose this toast to _____ and _____ wishing them joy and happiness in their future together.

There is a Jewish belief that 40 days before a child is born the name of the child's ordained mate (the *zivuk*) is announced by God.

Here's to _____ and _____. I wish you every success in your future and every happiness in your marriage.

Here's to the bride and groom. May you have a lifetime of love and an eternity of happiness.

> In Great Britain it is still considered good luck when a black cat crosses a bride's path on her way to the church.

_____ and _____ , I toast you: May you always be as happy as you are today.

It is an honor and pleasure to be asked to toast the bride and groom. Please stand and join with me: _____ and _____ , we wish you long life, good health, and a prosperous future.

We all raise our glasses to you as we toast your future. May the joy and happiness of this day remain with you throughout your married life. God bless you both.

> When a Korean bride and groom marry, ducks are included in the wedding procession because they mate for life.

Here's to the health of the happy pair;
May good luck follow them everywhere;

And may each day of wedded bliss
Be always as sweet and joyous as this.

I wish you health and I wish you wealth. May fortune be kind to you, and happiness be true to you for as long as you both shall live.

Let us toast to the health of the bride;
Let us toast to the health of the groom;
Let us toast to the person who tied;
Let us toast to every guest in the room.

May "for better or worse" be far better than worse.

It is an honor to be with you here today to witness your marriage ceremony and to share your joy. _____ and _____ , my heartiest congratulations, and may all your troubles be little ones.

When Princess Elizabeth married the Duke of Edinburgh in 1947, their wedding cake was 9 feet high and weighed 500 pounds. It was made with four tiers supported by silver pillars.

A toast to love and laughter and happily ever after.

_____ and _____ , may your love be as endless as your wedding rings.

May the road you now travel together be filled with much love and success.

After a Chinese wedding ceremony, the groom's parents host a tea service where the bride and groom pay tribute to their families. First, they bow to heaven, then to their heart, and then to their ancestors. Then, they bow to their grandparents and parents, serving each tea. In return, they receive jewelry and money.

_____ and _____ , congratulations on your wedding day, and my sincere wishes go with you both.

Chapter 2

Contemporary Toasts to the Bride and Groom

The toasts found here are examples of the contemporary phrasings being used today. They are more creative and personalized than the traditional toasts and have a lovely conversational quality about them that speaks straight from the toaster's heart.

Many of these toasts are appropriate as written, but those that give quite personal details about the couple should be used for inspiration for your own words.

During the 18th century and much of the 19th century, any toasts offered to women were called "sentiments."

Contemporary toasts to the bride and groom

To precious moments of togetherness, countless hours of sunshine and laughter, days of indescribable joy and celebration. May each morning be a happy surprise as you awake in each other's arms to discover that you love each other even more than the day before. To our newlyweds!

_____ (the bride), I've known you since the day you were born. I'll never forget that morning when your Dad and I wore a groove into the hallway outside the delivery room as we paced away the hours. And when the nurse laid you in your Dad's arms, I cried just as hard as he did. You were an incredibly beautiful baby, _____ (the bride). Over the years I've kept tabs on you—noting all your accomplishments, from your first piano recital to your graduation with honors from USC. And weren't you a lucky girl to choose that school, because that's where you met this guy. (Looks at groom with a smile.) I can't imagine what you saw in him—just because he happens to be a handsome attorney with a bright future, and just because he happens to adore you. I've only known you for about a year _____ (the groom), but I've got to say that even if _____ (the bride) were my own daughter, and I feel as if she is, I couldn't be more pleased with her choice. I'm proud and happy for you both and I wish you a future filled with all the joy you both deserve. Here's to _____ and _____.

To Fate that brought you together and to Love that will keep you happy forever. Congratulations and God bless.

> It's a Dutch tradition for a bride to carry a special handkerchief on her wedding day for catching her tears. This handkerchief is later passed down to the bride's eldest daughter for good luck.

What is true love? Lasting love? It's the kind of love we see between _____ and _____. Their love is unselfish, caring, and giving, and they have one of those rare love relationships that touches all our hearts—reminding us of what true love should be. _____ and _____, we toast your love, and we wish you joy and happiness in your married life. To _____ and _____.

I would like to propose a toast to _____ and _____. Your ceremony was filled with some of the most beautiful music I've ever heard. My wish for you is that your marriage will be as melodic and harmonious as the music we've heard today. May the music of your love overcome any discords that come your way. To a lifetime of joy and harmony.

A toast to _____ and _____. May you never be too old to hold hands, and may you say "I love you" every day.

> It is a Belgian tradition for a bride to carry a handkerchief embroidered with her name; this handkerchief is eventually framed and displayed in the couple's home until the next family bride adds her name and carries it down the aisle.

[Holding a pair of scissors.] I would like to propose a toast to _____ and _____ . I have here a pair of scissors. As we all know, there are two separate blades on a pair of scissors, but unless they work together, they are worthless. Although you are two unique individuals, may you have the joy and harmony of working together like a well-oiled pair of scissors. May all your dreams come true. To _____ and _____ .

_____ and _____, today is the start of something wonderful, a brand-new life, a beautiful beginning. Here's to a future filled with romance, delight, sharing, laughter, and great adventure as your love grows with each day. To your beautiful beginning!

It is estimated that 90 percent of American grooms wear wedding rings.

Mark Twain said, "It usually takes me more than three weeks to prepare a good impromptu speech," and it takes me even longer than that. _____ (the groom), when your parents asked me a month or so ago if I would like to offer a toast on this joyous occasion, I felt honored. And indeed it is an honor to toast you on this your wedding day. But like Mark Twain, I struggled with my thoughts because there is so much I would like to say. To begin with, I must tell you that when I heard you were engaged, my heart leaped with joy—I was so sure you two were meant for each other. Not only because you have so much in common— your compassionate hearts, your love of nature, and your shared interest in the field of medicine, but because your differences complement each other so beautifully as well. While _____ (the groom) is researching on the Internet for hours at a time, I'm sure _____ (the bride) will slip into her studio and enjoy time at the easel, creating another one of her delightful watercolors. Then, you'll come together again for one of those quiet times you've come to love as you walk hand-in-hand through the osprey sanctuary in back of your apartment. Oh, don't look so surprised—we know about those walks (as he smiles at the bride and groom). And just watching you two, it's easy to see how deeply you love each other. In fact, your love spills over and touches everyone around you, which is why it's such a joy for us to be here today. We will all leave here today with a new softness in our hearts and a fresh love and appreciation for our own spouses, all because of you. I wish I had the eloquence to express the joy I feel for you today. All I can say is this: _____ and _____, hold tight to each other and celebrate your love every day, and may each new day bring more joy than the last.

_____ and _____, today is the first day of the rest of your life. A life filled with joy and adventure as your love encompasses every aspect of your lives. Your partnership will be amazing. Every one of us here who knows you as individuals can't wait to see what you accomplish together as a team. We promise to encourage you and support you along the way, and we'll always be there for you when you need us. To _____ and _____.

An African bride in Kenya or Nigeria often braids her hair for her wedding day, forming the braids into a crown-like adornment on top of her head.

To a couple destined for a world of success, not only in life, but in love. Congratulations and good luck, my friends!

Please join me as we toast _____ and _____.
May your life together be filled with joy, bathed in love, and nourished by each other's care.

The most extravagant toast ever recorded was that offered to Marc Antony by Cleopatra when she dropped two perfect pearls into her wine and drank them down. The extravagance of her toast outweighed the cost of all the other banquet expenses combined.

_____ and _____, my dear friends, I speak from my heart when I say: May you have the strength to change those things that can be changed; may you have the patience to live with those things that cannot; and may you have the wisdom to know one from the other. My prayers and best wishes go with you both!

I would like to propose a toast to _____ and _____.
What a perfect day—your wedding day! You've waited a
long time for this, and it all went off without a hitch. In fact,
the ceremony was truly glorious and this reception is an
occasion we'll remember for years. I've never seen two
people so in love—in fact, your love casts a glow over all of
us. My wish for you is that as you look back on this day, and
as you face your future together, your love will continue to
glow for all the years to come. To a blessed life as husband
and wife.

> The peace of God came into my life when I
> wedded her.
> —Alfred, Lord Tennyson

_____ and _____, today is a day of new
beginnings. First of all, this is the day you embark on your
new life together as husband and wife. This is also the day
you establish a new home together, filled with laughter, joy,
sharing, and compromise. You will also experience new
family relationships, not only as your own unique family
unit, which may expand in the years to come as you have

your own children and grandchildren, but new relationships
because today you have also become part of each other's
families. Please stand as we toast _____ and
_____. To new beginnings.

As we toast you, _____ and _____,
I'd like to suggest a recipe for a happily married life: Take a
pound of tenderness. Mix it together with a tablespoon of
joy and a cup of laughter. Add a pinch of patience and a
sprinkling of kindness. Simmer slowly, watching carefully so
that it never comes to a boil. Strain it through a sieve of
tolerance, and you'll have a pudding as sweet and lasting as
your love. Please raise your glasses. To _____
and _____.

I can say without reservation that this has been the most
beautiful wedding I've ever attended, and never have I seen
a couple more in love than you. I toast you and your
marriage: May your love be modern enough to survive the
times, and old-fashioned enough to last forever. God bless
you!

_____ and _____, everyone here joins me in this toast as we wish you a lifetime of happiness. May your love grow stronger with each day, and may your marriage be kept safe and sheltered beneath angels' wings. To _____ and _____.

> A rice cake is placed on the heads of the Tibetan bridal couple, thus conveying life, health, and wealth.

We are so honored to be here with you today, to share your joy and to bask in your love. This is a very special day, _____(the wedding date), your wedding day, the day you have looked forward to for so long. And to think that this is only the beginning— just imagine that! I wish you a lifetime of love, a happy home, and great success in all you do. May you share equally in each other's love, and may all your troubles be little ones. Congratulations to our newlyweds!

A toast to the bride and groom: May all your tomorrows be promises come true.

I'd like to recite something written by William Shakespeare hundreds of years ago—see if you don't agree with me that he could have been writing _____'s and _____'s love story.

"No sooner met, but they looked;
No sooner looked but they loved;
No sooner loved but they sighed;
No sooner sighed but they asked one another the reason;
No sooner knew the reason but they sought the remedy."

Well, they sought the remedy all right, and the remedy was marriage. _____ and _____, you had a whirlwind courtship, that's for sure. First, there was the chance introduction at the Miami conference, then those long walks around Castlewood Bay, the countless candlelight dinners, and finally, the proposal just three months ago today. Once you found each other in Miami, it was just as Shakespeare said, "No sooner looked but they loved." May we call it "love at first sight"? I think so. All I can say is that I'm so happy for both of you, and I wish you a lifetime of long walks and candlelight dinners. To _____ and _____.

Here's a toast to _____ and _____. I believe love can last forever and grow even stronger with time, and that's what I'm wishing for you today.

The significance of today's wedding cake is said to have evolved from a type of Roman cake called the *conferreatio,* which was broken on top of the bride's head as a symbol of fruitfulness.

I would like to propose a toast to our lovely couple—may the joy of your love grow deeper with each hour, may your friendship grow closer each day, and may your marriage grow richer each and every year. I love you both. Cheers!

Please join me in a toast to the bride and groom. May the unbridled joy you feel today be but a pale shadow of that which is to come. Congratulations to you and God bless your marriage.

The heart that loves is forever young.
—Greek proverb

_____ and _____, your rings are beautiful. Hold them up for everyone to see. (After the bride and groom have held up their ring fingers for all to see, take the couple's ring hands in your own.) Their rings are circles, shining symbols of the deep, enduring happiness that comes from a lasting love and the fulfillment of a dream. (Release their hands and pick up your toasting glass.) I toast you _____ and _____ . May the endless circles of your wedding bands always be the symbols of your endless love.

Please stand with me as we honor our newlyweds with a toast: I wish you joy of heart, peace of mind, and the beautiful blessing of love.

To _____ and _____. May you always be there for each other, partners in marriage as husband and wife; may the sun shine brightly on your lives; and may you always be as happy as you are today.

Here's to _____ and _____ and a lifetime of gentle sunshine and sweet eternal love.

In days of old, the bride came to her husband with a dowry, but if the father of the bride disapproved of the groom, he refused to contribute to his daughter's dowry. Many of the villagers felt sorry for the bride and "showered" her with goods so that she would have an adequate dowry. Hence, our present-day custom of hosting a shower for the bride.

Thank you for letting us share in the joy of this special day and for allowing us to bask in the warmth of your love. We wish you a hundred years of sunshine and laughter; good fortune and good health; and, most of all, eternal devotion to each other. Here's to _____ and _____.

Ladies and gentlemen, it is now my pleasure to propose a toast to _____ and _____. May your marriage have every season of happiness: summers filled with cloudless skies and bubbling laughter, autumns filled with golden color and encouraging smiles, winters filled with crystal beauty and comforting hugs, and springs filled with soft rains and glorious new hope for the future.

Ladies and gentlemen, it is my pleasure to propose a toast to the bride and groom: May this day always live in your hearts, and may it be just the beginning of your beautiful forever together. Go with our love and Godspeed!

What is important is that one is capable of love. It is perhaps the only glimpse we are permitted of eternity.

—Helen Hayes

Here's to _____ and _____. May your married life be full of the same joy and happiness you feel at this moment. May your love grow even stronger every day, filling your future until it is overflowing with immeasurable joy.

Life is so much better when it's shared, and I'm so glad you found each other. May your marriage be bright and happy because of the very special joys that come with living… giving…caring. Here's to _____ and _____.

_____ and _____, how's married life so far? Is this an incredible day, or what? And it's only the beginning. Just think—there's a future still waiting for you out there, full of this same kind of joy and happiness, and it all began just an hour ago with those simple words, "I do." Memorize this day—this once-in-a-lifetime day—and appreciate every nuance, every emotion, every joy. And then, as your days turn to months, and your months to years, don't forget to experience the moment—those special moments in a marriage when you stop to enjoy the little things, those little pleasures so often taken for granted—the lavender sunset, the fragrance after the rain, the gentle caress and comforting touch. Here's to _____ and _____ and a lifetime of sweet, precious memories.

The custom of weaving a circlet of orange blossoms for the bride's head came to America from Spain, France and England in 1820; one was worn by Mary Hellen at a WhitHouse wedding when she married the son of President John Quincy Adams. The symbolism of the orange blossom is said to be that of virginity and the promise of fertility.

A toast to the happy couple: To a long, beautiful married life together, filled with peace, purpose, and prosperity.

May all your hopes and dreams come true and may the memory of this day grow even dearer with each year. To our newlyweds!

Robert Browning wrote, "What's all the earth compared with love?" There's nothing to compare with the kind of true love we see here today. _____ and _____, it's obvious that you're deeply in love, and it's a potent kind of love. Imagine what would happen if we could bottle it and pass it out to everyone we meet. To _____ and _____. May the power of your love bring you lasting happiness.

May you always share the kind of love and joy you feel today. _____ and _____, here's to a beautiful life.

Many African tribes marry a couple by binding their wrists with plaited grass.

A wedding consists of many things: ribbons and rings, music and vows, flowers and lace. But what would it all mean without it's essence: your love and commitment to each other. That's why this day is special, and as I offer this toast to you, _____ and _____, I do so with my sincere congratulations and this wish: that your love and commitment to each other this day will bring you all the good, sweet things a marriage should bring. To _____ and _____.

_____ and _____, it is said that the greatest happiness is sharing one life and one love forever. Here's to the greatest happiness. It has occurred to me that certain people just seem destined to find each other, and I know that everyone in this room realizes this is true with _____ and _____. Not only do they understand and believe in each other, but they fill each other's needs and support each other's dreams. As a matter of fact, all the little nooks and crannies of their lives seem to fit together perfectly. To two lucky people who found each other in time!

In the Philippines, a silken cord or string of flowers, also called a nuptial tie, is wound around the necks of the bride and groom in the form of a figure eight, the sign of infinity.

Ladies and gentlemen, it is a pleasure to propose a toast to the newlyweds. _____ and _____, I wish for you three things: warm moments shared together, thousands of tomorrows bright with love, and a lifetime of dreams come true. Cheers to the bride and groom!

A great writer by the name of Anna Barbauld has written these words: "The world has little to bestow where two fond hearts in equal love are joining." _____ and _____, there is nothing this world could offer that would compare with your love for each other. Your love was—from the very beginning a marriage-type love. Those of us who know you well recognized that from the start—perhaps even before you realized it yourselves. You see, when love is that special kind of love, the kind of love Ginny and I have had for each other for more than 30 years, we identify with it—we recognize it. It's a love money can't buy. We're so happy you found each other and we raise our glasses in a toast to you on this, your wedding day. To _____ and

_____.

> Most European countries follow the Roman tradition of celebrating weddings in the spring when homage was paid to the three divinities: Cres, Maia, and Flora.

Remember the moment you two fell in love? Those of us who know you well watched as the transformation took place. You couldn't hide it from us—not that kind of love! Every day was a new beginning for you. We noticed how you reached out to each other, took care to please each other, to fill every day with little surprises: the long phone calls; the love notes; the thoughtful little gifts; the warm, loving things you would say. Not that we were eavesdropping, mind you, but your mutual love was impossible to ignore—turning our hearts to the memories of our own courtship days. And today, we were all touched deeply as we witnessed your vows, and we will always remember the love, the joy, and the wonder of this special day. Cherish all these memories and hold them close to your hearts as you face a promising future together as husband and wife. Here's to

_____ and _____.

May every moment you share be sweet, may every today you share be happy, and may every tomorrow you share be a glorious new beginning. To _____ and

_____.

> One of the most unforgettable movie toasts of all time was proposed to Ingrid Bergman by Humphrey Bogart in *Casablanca*: "Here's looking at you, kid!"

Ralph Waldo Emerson once wrote that "all mankind love a lover," which is certainly true. And isn't that why we're so honored to be invited to this wedding—to share in the joy of this occasion, as we're doing now? Join me as we toast our newlyweds. May your love continue to grow and overflow, touching the lives of everyone you meet and all of us who know you. I love you. To _____ and

_____.

I'd like to propose a toast to _____ and _____, but first let me tell you a little story about _____ (the groom). I don't know if he'll remember this or not, but one

summer we took a Saturday and went to Disneyland with
our kids and the Taylors and their kids. Bryan (the groom)
must have been eight or nine, I think. Anyway, we got there
as soon as the place opened, bought our tickets, and were
standing there trying to decide which rides to stand in line
for first, when we realized that Bryan wasn't with us. We
looked around for him—we knew he couldn't have gone
very far. Meanwhile, Carol and Jamie wanted to head for
Magic Mountain, but we still couldn't find Bryan. Finally, I
found him behind one of the buildings watching some men
laying cement. He was fascinated with the way they were
troweling back and forth, giving the cement a smooth finish.
I said, "Bryan, what are you doing? We've been looking all
over for you." And do you know what Bryan said? He said,
"Could I just stay here for a little while and watch them?"
Here we'd paid $28 a piece, or whatever it was, to get into
the park, and all Bryan wanted to do was watch the workers
trowel the cement. We all had a good laugh over it and, of
course, looking back on it now, it's no wonder he turned out
to be one of our city's most successful building contractors.
Do you remember that, Bryan? Anyway, Bryan always knew
what he wanted and he hung in there until he got it, and he
knew what he wanted in a wife, too, and he held out until he
finally found the one who met his qualifications. _____
(the bride), you're a beautiful bride and a wonderful person

and everyone who knows you loves you. It's no wonder
Bryan asked you to be his wife! Congratulations to both of
you. To the happy couple!

Raise your glasses and join me in this toast to _____
and _____. May your tomorrows be filled with special
memory-making times yet to be shared—times of gentle
warmth and loving care.

> French newlyweds drink a reception toast
> from an engraved two-handled cup that is
> then passed along to their children and
> grandchildren in the years to come.

What is true love? True love is a love that's timeless, giving,
and growing. It's a love that's shared between two hearts
through any circumstance of life—through the hopes,
through the fears, through the joys, and the tears. What is
true love? It's a love that needs no words to explain it, but is
demonstrated through the hearts and lives of a man and
woman, It's the kind of love we see here today between
_____ and _____. May your love be
eternal.

When the bridal couple kneels during a German ceremony, the groom may "accidentally" kneel on the hem of his bride's gown to show that he'll keep her in order. Then, the bride may "accidentally" step on his foot when she rises, to reassert herself.

Please stand with me as we toast _____ and _____. Today your lives were joined as one. From this day forward, may your burdens be lighter, may your joys multiply tenfold, and may your lives be doubly rich because of the commitment you made today. Here's to the beautiful couple!

_____ and _____, we're really happy for you both, and we wish you all the joy you deserve from this day forward—the best is yet to come.

Chapter 3

Toasts by the Best Man

The best man usually offers the first toast to the bride and groom, and his toast is the only essential toast offered during the wedding reception, all others being optional. It is customary for the best man to reminisce a little about his friendship with the groom, relating interesting little stories and bits of humor, but always ending on a serious note. This toast should be delivered with as much poignancy and heartfelt sincerity as possible.

The best man is also expected to propose a "thank-you" toast to the bridesmaids on behalf of the bride and groom, unless the groom proposes this toast himself, in which case it is the best man's duty to reply to the groom's toast on behalf of the bridesmaids. An example of such a toast can be found on page 62.

A toast from the best man to the bride and groom

What an honor to be here, _____ and _____ , to be able to share the joy of this day with you as _____ (the groom's) best man. You know, it has been said that success in marriage is much more than finding the right person; it is a matter of *being* the right person, and I can say without reservation that you are so right for each other. When _____ (the groom) was in high school and college, he didn't date very much, at least not that I ever knew. He was very selective—preferring to spend his time on the basketball court or cruising over to the coast in his '56 Chevy that he'd worked so hard to restore, rather than to date someone who didn't meet the high standards he had set for his life's mate. Then he met you, _____ (the bride), and he was a goner. No more hours on the basketball court, and his cruisin' days were over…and why? Because there was nothing he'd rather be doing than spending time with you. You were the one! In fact, it couldn't be more obvious to everyone in this room that you were meant for each other, meant to spend your lives together. And as you set out together as partners on this journey called marriage, my prayers go with you that every day will be as joyous as this. Here's to you, _____ and _____.

> All mankind loves a lover.
> —Ralph Waldo Emerson

I would like to offer the first toast to _____ and _____.
Few things endure through a person's lifetime like the

power of friendship, and _____ (the groom), I value our friendship. You've been that one rare friend in my life who has always been there for me, and we've been through a lot together, haven't we? I remember the time we scrounged around our dorm room hunting for enough loose change to at least buy a loaf of bread and a jar of peanut butter to get us by until the first of the month; and that winter when we went a whole semester with no wheels because neither one of us could afford to get our cars fixed—it's not great bicycling around campus in 20 degree weather. But looking back on it all, the sacrifices were worth it. We survived those years and so did our friendship, a friendship forged in laughter and maintained by trust. As you and _____ (the bride) begin your life together as a married couple, I pledge my continued friendship—whenever you need me—just holler, and I'll be there. Here's to a lifetime of joy and happiness.

As _____ (the groom's) best man, please join me in a toast to the newlyweds. Actually, I have no idea why I'm called the "best man" because, as far as I know, no one pays the least bit of attention to a man in my position. You hear comments such as, "Isn't the bride absolutely radiant?" or "Isn't the groom handsome?" But do you ever hear anyone say, "Wow, have you noticed the best man—isn't he a great looking guy?" Nooooooooo. In fact, one of the guests thought I was with _____ (the name of the catering service). Actually, I want you all to know that I've been an *outstanding* best man—who else could have calmed _____ (the groom's) nerves the way I did? Who else could have been such a wise counselor? Who else could have been such a reassuring voice in his ear as I stood beside him during the ceremony? And who else could have done such an awesome job of arranging the honeymoon, *and* keeping their honeymoon destination such a *fine* secret, I might add? Actually, now that I think about it, with such outstanding qualities as these, I can't help but wonder why I'm still single. But seriously, it has been an honor to serve as _____ (the groom's) best man, and it is a special privilege to offer the first toast to the bride and groom. Here's to _____ and _____.

> In Costa Rica, a "hoke of matrimony," which is a white cord, is looped around the necks of the bride and groom by the priest as a blessing for their future offspring.

_____ (the groom), when you asked _____ (the bride) to marry you, you made the best decision of your life. I've known you for nine years, and I've never seen you happier

than you've been since the day you found_____ (the bride).
I'm glad for you, buddy! And _____ (the bride), you
didn't do so bad yourself! What an awesome couple! May
the happiness within your hearts today be a mere foretaste
of the joys you'll experience in the years ahead. May all your
dreams come true. Here's to _____ and _____.

It is my privilege and honor to propose a toast to the
newlyweds. John Keats said, "A thing of beauty is a joy
forever; its loveliness increases; it will never pass into
nothingness." My wish for you, _____ and _____,
is that your marriage will be a thing of beauty and a joy
forever, always as beautiful as you are today, _____
(the bride). And may the loveliness of your marriage
increase with each year. Here's to the bride and groom.

Thanks, _____ (the groom), for allowing me to stand
beside you today as you married _____ (the bride). I
couldn't be happier for both of you. I was beginning to
wonder, though, if you'd ever give up the single life—you
seemed pretty content with it. I can remember the first day
I met you, when you were hired on as a programmer, and
my first impression was that you seemed to be a pretty quiet

guy—very quiet, in fact. Remember that first company Christmas party? As I recall, there were several single gals who crashed the party—I can't remember where they worked—I think for some company in the Fremont building across the street. Anyway, they got to enjoying themselves pretty good when one of them, who'd had more than a few too many glasses of wine, decided to impress everyone there—especially the single guys standing around—by doing cartwheels across the floor—just like she used to do when she was a cheerleader in high school. Well, she asked everyone to step back so she'd have enough room to perform her gymnastics. I happened to be watching _____ (the groom) at the time, and he stepped back all right—all the way back to the opposite end of the room, where he turned his back on the whole charade, picked up a paper plate and started making himself a turkey sandwich off the buffet table. Man, was I impressed! What a classic move! It reminded me of a Chinese proverb I picked up during my college days: "Outside noisy, inside empty." Well, the more I got to know _____ (the groom), the more I realized that he never did care much for empty-headed women. It's no wonder he fell for _____ (the bride), who's not only beautiful, but a very smart lady. _____ (the bride), of course I'm a little partial because I know him so well, but I think that you made a *genius* decision when you decided to accept _____ (the groom's) proposal. You've married a great man—a man of amazing inner strength and integrity, a compassionate man who truly cares about other people. He's earned my unreserved respect and admiration, and I consider it a privilege to be standing here today offering this toast. _____ (the groom), you've been an awesome friend to me these past six years. Thanks. And now to _____ and _____, a very simple toast: Be happy!

The chanting of the Seven Wedding Blessings takes place at the end of a Jewish wedding ceremony while the groom, and then the bride, sip from a cup of wine.

This is an especially happy occasion for me today, not only because _____ (the groom) has been my best friend since third grade, but because _____ (the bride) has been a dear friend to _____ (the best man's wife) and me for many years. Looking back on it now, it was a momentous day when _____ (the groom) happened to be home on spring break at the same time _____ (the bride) was here visiting her folks, and we finally had a chance to introduce them to each other. _____ (the best man's wife) and I had often talked about what a great pair you two would make, but we never seemed to be able to get you together at the same time until that fated day last March. Now, as you stand here before us as a married couple and we see how perfect you are for each other, it's a special blessing to me to have been the one who introduced you. (Addressing the wedding guests: "Can you imagine what their kids are going to look like?" The guests cheer.) I love you both, and I lift this toast to you: May your lives be filled with the same joy and happiness you feel today.

During a Japanese ceremony, the *Timbangan* ritual is performed, whereby the bride and groom sit on the lap of the bride's father, who is seated on a ceremonial wedding couch. The bride's mother then asks the father which one is heavier. He replies that they are the same weight, signifying that, from then on, the bride and groom will be loved and treated equally by the parents.

As I stand here to honor our newlyweds, I think of these words written many years ago by an unknown author: "Time flies, suns rise, and shadows fall. Let time go by. Love is forever over all." My wish for you, _____ and _____ , is that your love will be forever over all, always abiding over the circumstances you will face as a married couple. To your forever-type love.

As I stand here today offering this toast to the handsome newlyweds, I can't help thinking of the saying: "Always a bridesmaid, never the blushing bride." They could change that to say: "Always the best man, never the blushing groom." Do you know that I've stood as the groom's best man four times since last summer? If this keeps up, I'll have to hire myself out as a professional. Actually, I can tell you why I'm still a bachelor at age _____ (the age of the best man)—because I've never met anyone like _____ (the bride). _____ (the groom), you done good, buddy! You must feel like you've won the lottery. You're a beautiful couple, and I wish you only the best in your years ahead as husband and wife. Here's to _____ and _____.

In Mexico the bride and groom kneel before the altar as they each hold a lighted candle and the priest wraps a single silver cord around their necks.

_____ (the groom), I've never seen you happier than you are today, and it's all because of this wonderful woman sitting by your side. _____ (the bride), thank you for making my friend so happy. Please raise your glasses and join me in a toast to a lifetime of happiness for _____ and _____.

(With mock mourning) My dear friends, we are gathered
here today to say goodbye to our dearly departed brother,
_____ (the groom), who has left the land of the living
for that never-never land known as "married life." We tried
to warn _____ (the groom); we told him to be careful or
this very thing might happen, but would he listen? Noooooo.
We warned him that he'd be forced to give up all those
pleasurable rounds of golf because he'd be repairing the
roof or helping his wife clean house. We warned him that
he'd have to give up his carefree Saturday afternoons
shooting baskets with the guys because his wife would insist
that he follow her around as she spent his money at the
mall. And, of course, gone were the lazy Sunday afternoons
when he could kick back and watch a little football on the
tube—he would be spending them with his *in-laws* instead
(glances at the bride's parents). Well, we did the best we
could, but he wouldn't listen. For some crazy reason he was
convinced that the joys of married life would far outweigh
the pleasures of bachelorhood. Can you imagine that?
Seriously though, all of us who have come to know and love
_____ (the bride) understand his reasoning completely.
_____ (the bride), you are so perfect for _____
(the groom), and I know you'll fill his days with more joy

and contentment than he could have found in a thousand rounds of golf or a hundred games of one-on-one. _____ (the groom), you've finally found the right woman, and we're happy for you. Here's to _____ and _____ and the joys of married life.

🜜

Benjamin Franklin said, "A single man is an incomplete animal. He resembles the odd half of a pair of scissors." _____ and _____ , it was destiny for you two to meet and fall in love—it couldn't have been any other way. Following Ben Franklin's train of thought a bit further— you're like a perfect pair of precision scissors. Your lives blend together so beautifully—a perfect meld, with your common interests and your uncanny abilities to meet each other's needs. As a matter of fact, I think you're exactly what a married couple should be—a team who accomplishes so much more together than you could have ever done as individuals. I'm so glad you found each other. Here's to _____ and _____ .

Korean couples make their vows silently as they bow to each other.

There are those who say the single life is the only way to go. They think the single life is more glitzy, more glamorous, and a lot more fun than being married. But let me tell you, having been converted from a bachelor to a married man myself, that so-called glitz and glamour is all flash—no substance. _____ and _____ , as you leave the single life behind and begin a beautiful journey together as husband and wife, I know you'll find that the rewards of marriage are the most valuable. To the joys of married life!

Is everyone enjoying themselves? Is this a great occasion, or what? Of course, most of us who know _____ (the groom) well thought this day would never come. We were all sure he was a confirmed bachelor, until he met _____ (the bride), of course. Actually, you can thank me for that. In fact, I feel like a real matchmaker. You see, I had been nagging at _____ (the groom) to come with me to the fitness club, just to try it out—you know. I was sure that once he got into the fitness thing he'd really like it. Well, after a year of nagging at him, I finally pulled him away from his computer one night and dragged him over to the club. But was he impressed? Not at all. He said he preferred riding his mountain bike and swimming laps at his parents' pool. So, admitting defeat, I gave up on him. Then, the strangest thing happened. Suddenly he decided he liked working out after all and, not only did he join the club, but he was over there four or five nights a week. I couldn't figure it out until I tagged along with him one night and noticed _____ (the groom) spending most of the time hanging out at the service counter talking to one of the gals who worked there—a gorgeous brunette by the name of _____ (the bride). And, of course, we all know what that led to—wedding bells! So, you have me to thank for this fantastic day! Seriously, _____ and _____, I couldn't be happier for both of you. You're a perfect couple, and I'm honored to have served as your matchmaker! Please join me as I toast _____ and _____.

Tip: Be sure your toast always includes the bride. Don't get carried away toasting the groom, who may be your best friend, and neglect to mention the bride.

A toast from the best man to the bridesmaids (on behalf of the bride and groom)

Ladies and gentlemen, it is now my pleasure to propose a toast of thanks and good wishes to the bridesmaids, not only on my behalf but on behalf of the bride and groom, as well. Your beauty brightened the ceremony; your smiles graced the platform; and your flawless performance enhanced the service with a lovely dignity. Thank you for everything you've done to help make this such a special day for

_____ and _____. Please join me in a toast to our

beautiful ladies!

A toast on behalf of the bridesmaids (in reply to the groom's "thank-you" toast to the bridesmaids, which is included in Chapter 6)

On behalf of the bridesmaids, I raise my glass in a toast of

thanks to _____ (the groom) for the kind words he

expressed toward _____ (the bride's) attendants. _____

(the groom) was so preoccupied with his beautiful bride,

I'm surprised he even noticed the bridesmaids, much less

how lovely they all looked in their _____ (color of the

bridesmaids' gowns) gowns. Actually, I was enormously

impressed with their contribution to the ceremony—of

course, I'm still a bachelor so my thinking may be a bit

skewed, but as they preceded the bride down the aisle, I

don't think I've ever seen a more stunning parade of women

in my life. On their behalf, I thank you.

It is an old English and Scottish tradition to pour a kettle of boiling water on the threshold of the bride's home as she leaves for the church. This is known as "warming the threshold," ensuring good luck.

Chapter 4

Toasts by the Father of the Bride

Up until the beginning of this century, it was the bride's father who usually delivered the first toast. Although this honor now falls on the best man, the bride's father still has the option of offering a touching toast to his daughter and her new husband. He may deliver this toast as the bride's father, or on behalf of himself and his wife. The father of the bride, as host, may also wish to propose a toast to the members of the wedding party, the guests, and his new in-laws, welcoming them into the family.

Marriage by capture was still legal in England until the 13th century.

A toast to the bride and groom

All the years _____ (the bride) was growing up, we knew that someday this day would come—her wedding day. This

is a very special day for us, as well as for _____ and
_____ , because it's a dream come true. You see,
_____ (the bride), it means so much to us to know
you've found the right guy and to see you so happy. Go with
our blessing, and may all your dreams come true.

_____ and _____ , they say that when a child finds
true love, the parents find true joy. Well, _____
(bride), you and _____ (groom) have definitely found
true love in each other, and Mom and I are overjoyed for
you both. If you ever need us for anything—anytime,
anywhere—you know we'll be there for you.
Congratulations to both of you, and let's get on with the
grandchildren!

> Let there be spaces in your togetherness.
> —Kahlil Gibran

_____ (the bride), what a delight you've been to Mom
and me. Every age and every stage of your growing-up years
brought us special joy. You've given us so much happiness,
and today we want you to know how very much you're
loved. It's time for you to leave your Mom and Dad now,
take this fella by the hand, and live with him for the rest of

your life. We hope and pray you'll be as happy as you have made us. Here's to _____ and _____.

❧

_____ and _____ , there are no words to adequately express the happiness and exhilaration we feel in our hearts today. _____ (the bride's mother) and I are absolutely overjoyed with your marriage, and if you two can be even half as happy as _____ (the bride's mother) and I have been, you'll have it made! Believe me...the day I married _____ (the bride's mother) was the luckiest day of my life. There's nothing quite like being married to a good woman. _____ and _____ , here's to a lifetime of happiness!

❧

I would like to propose a toast to _____ and _____ . I have never been more sure of anything in my life than I am of your marriage. At the end of the ceremony, when you turned to face us and were introduced as Mr. and Mrs. _____ , you were a picture I'll never forget—such a perfect match. _____ (the bride), the greatest thing we could wish for you and _____ (the groom) is to be as happily married as your mom and I have been, but I would like to add something more. This woman here (he places his arm around his wife's shoulder) is the reason why our marriage has been such a happy one. It's a good wife that makes a good marriage, and although I may be a bit prejudiced, _____ (the groom), you have married a *good* wife. Please rise and lift your glasses with me as we drink a toast to _____ and _____. To a long and happy married life.

_____ (the bride), do you remember when you were little and I used to read you a bedtime story every night? You always loved the fairy tales about princesses and knights in shining armor. Well, honey, today you're a beautiful princess yourself, and you've married your knight in shining armor. Here's to _____ and _____ and their "happily ever after."

The term "honeymoon" came from the early European custom of the married couple drinking wine made of honey for a month after their marriage. A month was then known as a "moon," so this time became known as the "month of honey" or "honey-moon." It's too bad most couples don't have a "month of honey" these days; they need it to recover from the stress of planning a wedding!

_____ (the bride's mother) and I would like to welcome you all here today and tell you how pleased we are to see our daughter looking so happy. Of course, we have lost a daughter today, but we entrust her to _____ (the groom's) care without reservation, knowing how he loves her and wants only the best for her. We've gotten to know _____ (the groom) pretty well over the last few months, and we're convinced that he's the right man for _____ (the bride). He has all the attributes we could have hoped for, and more. He's an honest, sincere man of integrity—charming, reliable—what can we say? He just couldn't be a greater guy! I know you all agree, so please stand with me as we wish them a happily married life together. To _____ and _____.

During the Ch'ing Dynasty (1644-1911) weddings had feasting, puppet shows, and musicians. The bride's gown was embellished with pomegranates, butterflies, and orchids.

A toast to his daughter, the bride

_____ (the bride), I'll never forget the day you were born. I was filled with joy and wonder as I looked down into your precious little face. It was the first day of our new life together—you, your mother, and I—full of hopes, dreams, and possibilities for your future. Today is another special day—a day that marks the start of your new life together with _____ (the groom). May your future be as bright with hope as the day you came into our lives. To the beautiful bride, my daughter, _____ (the bride).

Honey, you're "Daddy's Little Girl." You know that, don't you? You always have been and you always will be, even though you're a married woman now and you've left our home to live forever with _____ (the groom). You and _____ (the groom) will start a family of your own, and someday I'll be a grandpa to your own little ones—at least I hope that will happen, but even then you'll still be my little girl. It's hard to let go—I'm sure you know that—we've always been so close. But go with my blessing, be happy, and God bless you both.

The concept of romantic love is a fairly recent idea; in early history marriages were arranged by the parents.

I would like to propose a toast to my daughter. Although it's hard to believe when we see her here today, so elegant and gorgeous in her beautiful wedding gown, with her hair all done up that way and all—she used to be quite a tomboy. Oh, man—did she worry us sometimes. She could climb a tree or ride a horse or play goalie better than half the boys in town, and you loved it, didn't you _____ (the bride)? Mom would buy you barrettes and ribbons for your hair, hoping you'd doll yourself up a little, but by dinnertime your hair would be back in its braid, fastened with a rubber band. _____ (the groom), you never knew her when she was in her tomboy stage, but believe me, there's been quite a transformation. Just look at her—wow! To my beautiful daughter on her wedding day. Thanks for the memories!

A toast to his new son-in-law, the groom

_____ (the groom), welcome to our family. We've already grown to love you as our own son, and we wish you and _____ (the bride) a joyous future as you begin your lives as husband and wife. Here's to my new son.

In Old China, red was the color of love and joy—the color of the bride's gown, the ceremony candles, and the rosebud tucked into her groom's lapel.

I would like to propose a toast to our new son-in-law. You know it is said that to lose a daughter is to gain a son, and we're proud to have you as part of our family. I might mention that, in our case, not only have we gained a son, but a telephone! Her phone bills will be coming to *your* house now—praise God! But seriously, as her parents, we think your decision to marry our daughter was the best decision you'll ever make in your life. Here's to you, _____ (the groom).

_____ (the groom), welcome to our family. We think _____ (the bride) made a perfect choice—well, we hope not *too* perfect, because that would be pretty dull. You know, there is an expression: "A man who can be a hero to his wife's relatives can face the world without fear." Not only are you _____ (the bride's) hero, but you're ours, as well. We couldn't be more pleased about this marriage, and we're happy to have you as our son.

A toast to the members of the wedding party, the guests, and his new in-laws

I would like to thank the members of the wedding party for their willingness to participate in _____ and _____'s special day. I would also like to propose a toast to all our guests—thank you for coming. Your presence has graced this celebration. And finally, a special toast to _____ (the first name of the groom's mother) and _____ (the first name of the groom's father). We feel blessed to have you as part of our family, and our hope is that our friendship will grow even stronger as the years go by.

A toast to the guests and to the groom's family and friends

I would like to propose a toast to all of you, our honored guests, and especially to _____ (the groom's) family and friends. What a splendid day this has turned out to be— everything has gone so well, even the weather cooperated— such a happy day for all of us. _____ (the bride's mother) and I would like to thank you for coming to help us celebrate the marriage of our beautiful daughter _____

(the bride) and our handsome new son-in-law _____
(the groom). We have known quite a number of you for
many years, and others we have met for the first time today,
but we thank you all for coming. I toast you all!

> Love is of all passions the strongest, for it
> attacks simultaneously the head, the
> heart, and the senses.
> —Voltaire

Chapter 5

Toasts by the Father of the Groom

The father of the groom has the option of offering toasts to the bride and groom and to the hosts, the bride's parents.

A toast to the bride and groom

Our family has always been a circle of strength and love, and with every birth and every union, the circle grows. Every joy shared adds even more love and makes our circle stronger. Thank you, _____ (the bride), for joining our circle. We welcome you with open arms and, even though we've only known you for a short time, we have already grown to love you. We are so happy for both of you. Here's to _____ and _____.

I would like to propose a toast to _____ and _____. Someone suggested that I should give you newlyweds a word or two of advice. Well, I'm no great sage, that's for sure, but I do have one thing to say. A good marriage is like a good fire—to provide maximum warmth, the two logs should be kept close together, but to keep the fire *burning*, the logs need to be kept just a little bit apart so there will be breathing room. Here's to a marriage that burns warm *and* long.

> No displays of affection are allowed at a Buddhist wedding.

_____ (the groom), after all these years your mom and I were beginning to wonder if you would ever find the right girl. But last December when you casually asked if we might know of a good jeweler, we began to suspect that maybe you had finally found her. Mom and I didn't dare ask too many questions. After all, you could have been shopping for a Christmas gift—maybe a friendship ring or a gold chain— but something about your excitement made us wonder if maybe you weren't doing some serious shopping for an engagement ring. I can say, without doubt, that we've never seen you as happy as you've been since you started dating

_____ (the bride), and that Christmas Eve when you placed the ring on her finger, we were as overjoyed as we could be. _____ (the bride), welcome to our family. Here's a toast to our happy newlyweds.

This is a pretty emotional day for _____ (the groom's mother) and me because _____ (the groom) has finally taken himself a wife, and nothing could make us happier. When children marry, parents feel a blend of joy and sorrow—the door that closed yesterday reopens tomorrow with fresh dreams and memories to fill our hearts. We're overjoyed to have you as part of our family, _____ (the bride). God bless you both as you begin your new lives together as husband and wife.

By the time a girl in rural America had handstitched her 11th quilt, which usually took many years of work, she was declared ready for a suitor. Then she began work on her 12th quilt, known as the "wedding quilt." This 12th quilt was always conveniently finished just in time to use on her wedding night.

I would like to propose a toast to my son and his beautiful wife. Your love and commitment to each other have touched us all. May your love, which is so rich and sweet, fill your home. In fact, may your love overflow your hearts and spill out to others. To your friends, your family, your coworkers, your neighbors, and to all those you'll entertain in your home through the years. Here's to _____ and _____ , and your everlasting love.

There is an old English proverb that states: "A joy that's shared is a joy made double." _____ (the groom), your mom and I are so happy for you and _____ (the bride), and may your joy be doubled as you leave here today to begin your new life together as husband and wife. To our son and his new wife.

There couldn't be a better time than this to reflect on the pleasures of having a wonderful son like _____ (the groom). There have been times through the years when _____ (the groom's mother) and I looked at each other in wonder. How could we have been so blessed as to have a son like this? _____ (the groom), you've done nothing but make us proud—in the choices you've made through the years and the ways you worked so hard to fulfill your dreams. You've touched our lives deeply, and it's difficult to find the words to express the love and affection we have for you as our son. And, speaking of choices, you couldn't have chosen a more beautiful woman to be your wife. She's not only beautiful on the outside, but on the inside as well. You've done good, son, and your Mom and I toast you and _____ (the bride). May your marriage be filled with as much happiness as you've brought us through the years.

Some husbands are living proof that a woman can take a joke.
—Anonymous

It has been said that when children find true love, parents find true joy. _____ and _____ , you have certainly found true love, that kind of lasting love that makes a marriage a joy, the kind of love _____ (the groom's mother) and I have had for more than _____ years. Thank you for the joy you have brought us by the joining of your hearts and lives together this day. Here's to our son and his beautiful new wife.

_____ (the groom), congratulations on choosing such a wonderful woman to be your wife. When I look at _____ (the bride), I'm reminded of something Robert Burns wrote: "To see her is to love her, and love but her for ever, for nature made her what she is, and ne'er made anither!" To see _____ (the bride) is to love her, for she's a rare jewel, a one-of-a-kind treasure. Your mom and I are so happy for you both, and we welcome _____ (the bride) into our family with open arms. Here's to our son and his lovely new wife, _____ (the bride).

Raising a son is an interesting phenomenon; we've raised three, and each one is different. _____ (the groom) was always the adventurous one. I can remember when he was eight or nine years old, and _____ (the groom's brother) and _____ (the groom's other brother) were content playing Monopoly or building a fort in the backyard. _____ (the groom) wanted to go hike through Compton Wilderness Park to look for Grizzlies, or take a family raft trip down the Colorado River rapids, or go ice fishing when it was 10 below zero. He was a challenge all right, and you don't even want to hear about his teen years. He about wore us out! But looking back on it now, I can see that _____ (the groom) was the reason our family had so much fun through the years. If ever we resisted one of his adventurous new ideas, he always pushed, pulled, and prodded until we finally gave in to his plan. When we realized that _____ (the groom) was dating someone and that *this* time it might be serious, _____ (the groom's mother) and I wondered if the gal knew what she was getting into. But sure enough, as we got to know _____ (the bride), we realized that she's as crazy about the outdoors as _____ (the groom.) In fact, if ever there was a marriage made in heaven, this is it. Congratulations to our son and his brave new wife _____ (the bride).

> Unable are the Loved to die
> For Love is immortality.
> —Emily Dickinson

A toast to the bride's parents

I would like to take this opportunity to thank _____ (the bride's mother) and _____ (the bride's father).

You have been charming, gracious hosts and it is an honor to be related to you through the marriage of our children. I hope our friendship continues to grow through the years, and I know it will. Here's to _____ (the bride's mother) and _____ (the bride's father).

In 1840, Queen Victoria started a fad by wearing an all-white wedding gown. A few years later, Empress Eugenie, known as quite a fashion plate, wore a white gown when she married Napoleon III. Up until that time, the bride wore an ethnic wedding costume or the best dress she owned, which was usually her black "Sunday dress." Today, a white wedding gown has come to signify virginal purity.

Chapter 6

Toasts by the Groom

The groom has the option of proposing toasts to his bride, the parents, his grandparents, the guests, and the bridesmaids, unless he delegates this latter duty to his best man on his behalf. The groom's toast to his bride is usually short, poignant, and well thought out in advance.

A toast by the groom to his bride

I would like to propose a toast my wife, _____ (the bride). With this toast, I pass all my love from my heart to yours.

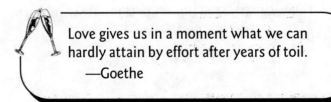

Love gives us in a moment what we can hardly attain by effort after years of toil.
—Goethe

My greatest treasures are all our yesterdays, but my greatest prize is our lifetime of tomorrows. To all our tomorrows.

This toast is to my beautiful wife. _____ (the bride), thank you for being so easy to love. Here's to a lifetime of quiet moments just for dreaming, laughing moments just for sharing, and tender moments warm with caring. To my bride.

A *chuppah*, used during a Jewish wedding ceremony, symbolizes the couple's new home. During Bible days, it was a specially decorated tent set up in the courtyard of the bride's family.

I would like to propose a toast to my best friend, my bride, _____ (the bride). I'm so glad I married my best friend. Because of our friendship, our marriage will be a comfortable relationship where we feel understood and accepted, always with each other's best interests at heart. Here's to my wife.

_____ (the bride), with this toast I offer you the gift of my eternal love, given with a free and open heart.

I would like to propose a toast to my wife. From this moment forward I will share my life with you as your husband, and my love for you will never change except to become deeper still as each day passes. To my wife, _____ (the bride).

A *shivaree* is a tradition that began during the Middle Ages in which the friends of the couple made a racket to embarrass the newlyweds on their wedding night. This is still a custom in many parts of our country today.

To my wife, _____ (the bride). You are a priceless treasure. I will admire you, protect you, love you, and hold you tenderly. Thank you for choosing me to be your husband.

As I lift this glass in a toast to my beautiful bride, we see that the glass is full. There may be times in our future, _____ (the bride), when the glass is only half-full, but when those times come, and they will, may the empty space be merely an opening, an opportunity to fill our lives with even greater hope. To our glorious future together as husband and wife. May our lives always be filled with joy even when our glasses are only half-full.

In Morocco, marriages are usually celebrated at the end of harvest, in the autumn.

I was warned ahead of time that you were the most beautiful bride the guests had ever seen, but I was blown away when I saw you walking down the aisle on your dad's arm. I agree, you *are* the most beautiful bride, and I can't wait to take care of you and spend my life with you.

I would like to propose a toast to my bride. Thank you for a chance to love and to be loved.

To my wife, _____ (the bride). You are my bride and joy.

In Poland, many reception guests pin money on the bride and groom to "buy a dance."

Today I married my best friend. To my wife.

To my bride, _____ (the bride), and a lifetime of sharing—sharing in every way—from the little things, such as reading the newspaper together on Sunday morning, to the big things, such as when to buy a house or when to have our first baby. May our shared lives multiply our joy.

A toast to my wife, _____ (the bride). When we arrived here today, we were two separate people, but now we are united as husband and wife. To one heart, one love, one life.

Many Japanese couples fly to the United States to have an American wedding, which, for them, is preferable to the formal, ornate, scripted Japanese ceremony.

_____(bride), you are incredible! I admire you for the way you've managed as a single mother. You carried the entire load yourself—the kids, the finances, your job. And you never complained. In fact, judging by your smile, anyone would think you didn't have a worry in the world. I want you to know that I'm here now to be your helpmate. I'll share the load from this day on—with great joy and all my love. To my wife!

_____ (the bride), did you know that no matter how dark the day, no matter how down my mood, when you walk into the room, the sun comes out? To my sunshine—the light of my life.

I would like to toast my bride. _____ (the bride), I've never told you this before, but that first time I met you when Jim introduced us, something happened inside my head. It was like a soft voice whispering to me, over and over: "She's the one—she's the one." And you were. I'm so glad we found each other. To my bride.

In the Middle Ages, the giving of a simple gold wedding ring constituted a legal marriage, even if no one else was there to witness it.

To my wife, _____ (the bride). May our marriage draw us closer and closer together, but may it never supersede our individuality. I love you just the way you are—please don't ever change.

I raise my glass in honor of my lovely bride. May our marriage bloom through every season—not only seasons of sunshine when everything seems to be going our way, but those seasons of darkness when our love and commitment must be strong enough to wait out the darkness until the sun breaks through again. With this toast I pledge my love through every season. To my wife.

I'd like to get serious here for a minute as I toast my bride. _____ (the bride), when I saw you in your wedding gown for the first time as you walked down the aisle, I wondered what I ever did to deserve such happiness. I am humbled and grateful to have you for my wife. My heart is full. Here's to you, _____ (the bride).

It's said to be good luck to find a spider on your wedding gown anytime during the wedding day.

When we recited our vows this morning (or afternoon or evening), you and I became "us." From this day on, everything we do, every decision we make, every thought will be for "us." To "us"—for now and forever.

_____ (the bride), we have only just begun to see what our love can be…to our unending future.

I would like to propose a toast to my bride on our wedding day. _____ (the bride), I'll remember this day for the rest of my life. It's been the most wonderful day—I feel so peaceful and full of joy. It's like a dream. I'm savoring every word, every emotion—hiding them away in my memory. Thank you for marrying me. Here's to my beloved wife.

To my wife, _____ (the bride). I'm going to fall in love with you all over again every day.

The kiss became part of the marriage ceremony as far back as early Roman times when it signified a legal bond that sealed contracts.

I would like to toast my lovely wife. _____ (the bride), let's live every day of our married life as if it were the last. Let's hold each other close every morning. Let's say "I love you" a hundred times a day. Let's not squander our moments, but spend them all on our love. To our beautiful tomorrows.

_____ (the bride), I love you so much at this moment—I'm almost overwhelmed by my feelings. I can't even begin to imagine the depth and breadth of my love for you after we've been married one year or five years or 50 years. How will I bear it? It's beyond my comprehension. To _____ (the bride).

May I live a thousand years and you a thousand and a day, for I couldn't bear to live without you. To my life, my future, my wife.

To my beloved wife—we've only just begun.

> The tradition of flower girls began in the Middle Ages. They preceded the bride down the aisle carrying tiny stalks of wheat—symbols of a fruitful and happy marriage.

I would like to propose a toast to my wife, _____ (the bride). I can't believe this long-awaited day has finally come and you are no longer my fiancée, but my wife. "Wife"—the most beautiful word in the English language. _____ (the bride), you are God's precious gift to me, my springtime, my hope, and my joy. You're everything that's good and pure and true, and I'm so blessed to be able to say that you're mine, to be able to love and cherish you for the rest of my days. To my wife.

_____ (the bride), you are joy to my heart and food to my soul. May our future be filled with laughter, sunshine, and our sweet, eternal love. To my soul mate—my wife, _____ (the bride).

I would like to propose a toast to my lovely bride, _____ (the bride). I love you more than yesterday and less than all our tomorrows.

It's lucky to see a dove, frog, goat, lizard, or lamb on your way to the wedding ceremony; but very bad luck to see a dog, pig, or snake.

To my beautiful bride, _____ (the bride). May our lives be beautiful together; may all our dreams come true, and may I give back to you the gifts of love you give me every day.

I would like to propose a toast to my bride. _____ (the bride), you are lovely, in every sense of the word. I love you, and I'm proud to be standing here today as your husband. Here's to my bride, _____ (the bride).

> Navajo Indian brides traditionally marry while facing east, in the direction of the rising sun.

The greatest happiness—the greatest gift possible—is to be able to share my life with you. Thank you for giving me this gift. To my wife, _____ (the bride).

Here's to the one who halves my sorrows and doubles my joys, my beautiful bride, _____ (the bride).

Note: You and your bride may also wish to compose private toasts to be delivered to each other once you've shed the crowds and finally arrive at your honeymoon destination. These toasts, if you choose to compose them, will be the most precious of all as you speak from the intimacies of your hearts.

A thank-you toast by the groom to the bridesmaids

_____ (the bride) and I would like to propose a toast to the bridesmaids. What a vision you made in your

_____ (color of the bridesmaids' gowns) gowns. We really appreciate your willingness to participate in our wedding and everything you've done to help prepare for this day. We can't thank you enough. Please join me in a toast to the bridesmaids.

Note: See the best man's toast of reply on behalf of the bridesmaids on page 62.

> The age-old tradition of the father giving away his daughter in marriage has survived from the times when a bride was actually sold to the groom, and her father handed her over to her husband in return for compensation.

A thank-you toast by the groom to the bride's parents

I would like to propose a toast to _____ (the bride's Mom and Dad). You have raised quite a daughter here (smiles at his wife). Thank you for entrusting her to me—I will do my best not to disappoint you. Thank you for accepting me into your family as your son and for providing us with such a memorable wedding day. We love you! To _____ (the bride's mother) and _____ (the bride's father).

In rural China, the groom's family always brings gifts to the bride's family in large wedding baskets filled with oranges, cooked chickens, cakes, and roast pig.

A toast by the groom to his parents

I would like to propose a toast to my parents. Mom and Dad, although it's really difficult for me to put my feelings into words, I want you to know how much I appreciate your love and encouragement through all the years. You've made a lot of sacrifices for me—especially when I was struggling to get through college—and I'll never forget it. You're the best parents a son could ever have, and you've set a wonderful example for me of what a really good marriage should be. Thank you for helping make our wedding day so special. To my Mom and Dad.

Chapter 7

Toasts by the Bride

The bride may propose a toast to her parents, her grand-parents, her groom's parents, or to her groom (but only if her groom has toasted her first). She may also toast her brides-maids, whether or not they have already been toasted by the groom or the best man.

A toast by the bride to her groom

For all the wonderful ways you've touched my heart, and for all the unexpected ways you've changed my life, I love you. To my husband.

To my husband, my best friend. With this toast I offer you all my love for all my life.

In Poland a bride usually wears an embroidered white apron over her wedding gown; guests discreetly tuck money into its pockets.

I would like to propose a toast to my husband, _____ (the groom). What a blessing to call you "husband." It took me a long time to find someone I wanted to marry. In fact, I searched for you all my life. Thank God, I finally found you. You have all the qualities I dreamed of in a husband—you're an honest man, unselfish, loving, caring, supportive, and my ideal in every way. To my godsend, my husband, _____ (the groom).

_____ (the groom), today our dreams came true as you and I became one. Here's to our future and a lifetime of new dreams yet to come. To my husband, _____ (the groom).

To my husband, _____ (the groom). May our marriage always be a safe haven from the world and a place of love and peace.

It is tradition for the mother of a Polish bride to give her daughter bread, salt and wine after she is married so that she will never lack the necessities of life.

I would like to propose a toast to my wonderful husband, _____ (the groom). Today is our beautiful beginning of a hundred years of happy tomorrows, and it is a celebration of the very best we have to offer each other. Here's to you _____ (the groom)—may all our dreams come true.

I would like to say a few words. You know, this wedding has been in the planning stages for more than a year. In fact, everything seemed to revolve around the plans. There were countless meetings with the photographer, the caterers, the florist, and the musicians, and there were hundreds of hours spent shopping and choosing, striving for the perfect gown or that perfect shade of lace. But today when I stood next to you, _____ (the groom), and recited my vows, I realized that all the plans, all the time, and all the anxieties paled in comparison to the essence of this day. Without you, _____ (the groom), the day would have no value, no meaning at all. To my precious husband, _____ (the groom).

I would like to propose a very simple toast to my wonderful husband: Thank you for making me your wife. I will always trust in your love and you can always trust in mine. To you, _____ (the groom).

> By all means marry; if you get a good wife, you'll become happy; if you get a bad one, you'll become a philosopher.
> —Socrates

To my husband and our shared future filled with peace and happiness.

_____ (the groom), it has been said that true love is the only glimpse of eternity we are given. From the first day we realized our love wasn't just a transient thing, but something eternal, I became filled with a heavenly joy and elation unlike any to be found on this earth. And this is just the beginning. To my husband and to our eternal love.

Young Amish boys playfully toss the groom over a low fence to symbolize his passage into a new life.

_____ (the groom), I will always remember the first time I saw you, the first time you held my hand, the first time you brought me flowers, the first time you kissed me good night. All these memories, and others too, are timeless treasures stored within my heart, to be relished and savored at will. But of all the memories, none can compare with those made here today—the expression on your face as my father walked me down the aisle, the sound of your voice as you recited your vows, your touch, your kiss, your smile. I will remember them until the day I die. To my husband, _____ (the groom). Thank you for the memories.

I would like to propose a toast to _____ (the groom). My dream was to find a man who would understand me without me uttering a single word, a man whose values and spirit matched my own—a soul mate. I finally found him. To my soul mate, _____ (the groom).

_____ (the groom), today is our wedding day and everything is beautiful and perfect and full of hope. But there will be days that are less than perfect and when they come along, let's remember this moment. Here's to my husband and the joy of spending *all* our days together.

Note: You and your husband may also wish to compose private toasts to be delivered to each other once you've shed the crowds and finally arrive at your honeymoon destination. These toasts, if you choose to compose them, will be the most precious of all as you speak from the intimacies of your hearts.

During a Greek Orthodox wedding ceremony, the best man, known as the *koumbaros*, places crowns, joined by a ribbon, on the heads of the couple. Then he switches the crowns three times, signifying the Holy Trinity; afterward, the bride and groom circle the wedding table, known as the *analogion*, three times.

A toast by the bride to her groom and to their parents

I would like to propose a toast to my wonderful husband, _____ (the groom), and to his parents who raised him to be the caring, responsible man of integrity he has turned out to be. They were always there for _____ (the groom), supporting him in every way possible. I would like to take this opportunity to thank them publicly for making me feel so loved and such a welcome member of their family. I would also like to toast my parents and to thank them for their love, their support, and their prayers. I'm so blessed to have such marvelous parents—and I especially thank you, Mom and Dad, for giving _____ (the groom) and me such a beautiful wedding day. Here's to _____ (the groom) and our parents.

I would like to propose a toast to my wonderful husband, _____, and to his parents. Thank you for raising him to be a loving man of high morals and compassion for others. I know you sacrificed to put him through college, and I thank you for that, too. He has become the man he is because of you. I toast you with my love.

A toast by the bride to her mother

I would like to propose a toast to my mother. I'm so blessed to have you for my Mom. Thank you for your unselfish love, your understanding, your loyalty. Through all the years, you've always encouraged me and believed in me, and you've been a wonderful example to me of the kind of wife and mother I'd like to be. Thank you. To my Mom.

Mom, please stand so everyone can see you. Isn't she beautiful? There is an old Jewish proverb that says, "God could not be everywhere and therefore he made mothers." Mom, you were always there for me, for as long as I can remember. Thank you for everything you've done for me, everything you've meant to me, everything you've sacrificed for me through the years. Here's a toast to my mother.

A toast by the bride to her parents

For the past year we've been caught up in the excitement of planning this wedding, and I'm so thankful to you both for all your help and support. Now I'd like to take this opportunity to tell you publicly how much you mean to me and how I appreciate all the special gifts you've given me: the gifts of your patience, your support, your sacrifice—all gifts I can never repay. But, of all your gifts, none are greater than your gift of *love*. Thank you, Mom and Dad.

Marry in May and you'll rue the day.
—Early European folklore

It's my wedding day, a perfect time to tell you how important you are to me and to thank you for all you've given me: a sense of the joy life can hold, the ability to forgive, and the capacity to love and be loved. As I leave here today as _____ (groom's) wife, I'll take these gifts with me, but I'll never forget that I'm your daughter. I love you.

A toast by the bride to her grandparents

I'm so glad my grandparents are here to share in the happiness of my wedding day. Your love has been a part of my life for as long as I can remember, and I know it will always be. Because of you, today seems even more beautiful. To my Nana and Pop-Pop.

A Jewish couple usually signs an elaborately embellished *ketubah*, or marriage contract, which is then hung in a prominent place in their home.

A toast by the bride to her grandmother

I would like to propose a toast to my Grandma. Nana, when I look at you, I see such a beautiful face. Do you know how many lives have been brightened by your smile, how many hearts have been warmed by your love? You have been a very special person in my life, and you always will be. I love you, Nana. Thank you for making my day so special.

A toast by the bride to her bridesmaids

I would like to propose a toast to my bridesmaids. Thank you for making my day so special—I love you all. Here's to

_____ , _____ , _____, and _____ (the first names of her attendants).

Most fingers of both hands have been used for wedding rings throughout history; however, the Christian tradition that began in 860 A.D. placed the wedding ring on the fourth finger of the left hand because it was believed that this finger is directly connected to the heart by the "vena amoris," or vein of love.

Chapter 8

Toasts With Religious Variations

Many families believe that the deep spiritual significance of marriage should not only be emphasized throughout the wedding ceremony itself, but throughout the reception as well, including the wording of the wedding toasts. Here is a collection of toasts that offer a variety of spiritual and religious phrasings, many of which have been inspired by the Bible. The majority of these toasts have general spiritual or Judeo-Christian overtones. Those that are appropriate for a specific religion, however, have been identified as such.

> Perfect love casts out fear.
> —I John 4:18

A toast by the groom to his bride

The Bible says that it is not good for man to be alone, and how I praise God for giving you to me. Before you came

105

into my life, I thought I was self-sufficient—and doing quite well, actually—but now I know that without you I was a mere shadow of the man God really wants me to be.

_____ (the bride), not only are you my best friend, but my strength and my inspiration—the power that propels my spirit day by day. You have filled a void in my life that I didn't even realize existed. To my wife—the wind beneath my wings.

> It was an old Dutch tradition for an engaged couple to cut their fingers and swallow each other's blood as a guarantee that they would be faithful to each other forever.

I would like to propose a toast to my wife. In the second chapter of the Song of Solomon, we find these words:

"My Beloved spoke, and said to me:

Rise up, my love, my fair one, and come away.

For, lo, the winter is past,

The rain is over and gone;

The flowers appear on the earth;

The time of singing is come,

And the voice of the turtle is heard in our land;

The fig tree putteth forth her green figs,

And the vines in blossom give forth their fragrance,

Arise, my love, my fair one, and come away."

_____ (the bride), thank you for marrying me. You are my beloved, my love, my fair one, and our time of singing has finally come. Arise, my love, and come away with me. To my bride.

> A Spanish groom gives his bride 13 coins (the giving of *modedas* or *arras*) to show his ability to support and care for her. Thirteen represents Jesus Christ and his 12 apostles.) At the ceremony, the bride carries them in a purse, or a young girl holds them on a pillow or handkerchief.

I would like to propose a toast to my beautiful bride. In the "love chapter," I Corinthians 13, we find these words:

"Love is patient, love is kind.

It does not envy, it does not boast,

It is not proud. It is not rude, it is not self-seeking, it is not easily angered.

It keeps no record of wrongs.

Love does not delight in evil but rejoices

with the truth. It always protects, always

trusts, always hopes, always perseveres."

_____ (the bride), this is Christ-like love, and it's the kind of love we have for each other. May our marriage always be filled with His love.

A Christian toast

> A Jewish wedding can not be held on the Sabbath (Friday after sundown until Saturday after sundown) or on any of the major Jewish religious holidays (Rosh Hashanah, Yom Kippur, Passover, Shavout, and Sukkot).

_____ (the bride), you are my strength, my treasure, my perfect one. I thank God for bringing me such a priceless gift. To my wife.

_____ (the bride), in the book of Genesis it is said that "a man shall leave his father and mother and be joined to his wife, and they shall become one flesh." Today we left our parents' homes to be joined together as husband and wife, to become one flesh. I thank God for His plan and I thank God for you, _____ (the bride). To my beautiful bride!

Many cultural traditions place the bride and groom under a canopy: The Jewish couple stands under a *chuppah*; a Greek couple stands under a *thalamos* (a bridal bower); Spanish and Brahmin brides and grooms stand beneath a canopy; and in the villages of Scotland, newlyweds are escorted beneath a floral bower from the church to their new home.

_____ (the bride), you are God's work of art. When I gaze upon your face, I am filled with awe and wonder at the absolute perfection He bestowed upon you. I thank God for entrusting me with such an exquisite treasure. To you, _____ (the bride).

I would like to propose a toast to my wife. In the book of Proverbs it is said that "a virtuous woman is a crown to her husband," and this is a fitting description of you, my angel, my beloved bride. Not only are you a virtuous woman, but a Godly woman, as well. I thank God for you, _____ (the bride). Here's to my bride and to our future.

To my wife, _____ (the bride). May our Higher Power give us the ability to accept the things we cannot change, the courage to change the things we can, and the wisdom to know the difference.

Inspired by the Serenity Prayer

> Drinking rituals are the central features of Japanese and Chinese weddings. The commitment of the couple, or sharing of their vows, is demonstrated publicly by sharing drinks together. Japanese couples drink sake from the same cup while Chinese couples share wine, sometimes mixed with honey, from two cups tied together with a red silk thread.

The book of Proverbs states that "Whoso findeth a wife findeth a good thing." _____ (the bride), not only are you a "good thing," but the *best* thing that's ever happened to me. To my wife, _____ (the bride).

_____ (the bride), these words are written in the book of Ecclesiastes:

"To everything there is a season, and a time to every purpose under the heaven: a time to be born, and a

time to die; a time to plant, and a time to pluck up
that which is planted...a time to weep, and a time to
laugh; a time to mourn, and a time to dance; a time
to cast away stones, and a time to gather stones
together; a time to embrace and a time to refrain
from embracing...a time to love, and a time to hate;
a time of war, and a time of peace...I know that,
whatsoever God doeth, it shall be for ever; nothing
can be put to it, nor any thing taken from it: and
God doeth it, that men should fear him."

_____ (the bride), our time has finally come—our
wedding day—our time to laugh, our time to dance, our
time to love, our time to embrace. I thank God for bringing
us together in His perfect time. To my precious wife,
_____ (the bride).

Here's a toast to my bride, _____ (the bride), and to a
lifetime of loving and serving each other, just as our hearts
long to love and serve God.

> Many Scandinavian and Eastern Orthodox
> brides wear a wedding crown that usually
> belongs to the church, thus becoming
> "queen for a day."

I would like to propose a toast to my bride, _____
(the bride). Our God has created us as bride and
bridegroom, and because of Him, we rejoice. May our
marriage always be a testimony to His love and providence.

A Jewish toast

From the moment I invited Christ into my life at the age of
_____, I began to pray that He would lead me to
the one He wanted me to marry. All through college and
during my three years of internship, I kept looking and
praying and searching. Then, one day, about a year ago, I
finally found her, and from that first moment I saw her, I
knew. And you knew, too, didn't you,
_____ (the bride)? There's nothing that
can compare with the joy of knowing you've found the right
one—the one God has saved just for you. It isn't just a
"love-at-first-sight" kind of thing, although it certainly was
that, but it's that deep sense of peace knowing that God has
brought you together. I thank God for saving you just for
me, _____ (the bride). Here's a toast to my
precious wife.

A Christian toast

The tradition of creating a bell-like sound by clinking glasses together during a toast is said to have begun during the Christian era as a way to scare away the devil, who was believed to be terrified by the sound of bells.

_____ (the bride), may our home be a safe haven filled with God's love; may our marriage be a testimony of God's grace and blessing; and may our future always be as bright and beautiful as our wedding day.

A toast by the bride to her groom

To my husband, _____ (the groom). May our marriage always be a testimony of our deep and abiding love for each other and for our Heavenly Father.

_____ (the groom), in the book of Genesis, Adam said, "This is now bone of my bones and flesh of my flesh; she shall be called Woman." Today we became joined as husband and wife, and we are no longer two individual

people, but joined as one. _____ (the groom),
God has willed this, and He has given me to you to be your
"Woman" from this day forward. What a lovely plan *that* is!
Thank you, Lord. To my husband, _____
(the groom).

> Bagpipers often entertain at Scottish
> weddings, where the Highland fling is
> usually performed.

To my husband, _____ (the groom). May God bless
our marriage and make us pleasing to Him every day.

To my husband, _____ (the groom). May our marriage
be protected by God's love.

I would like to propose a toast to my husband, borrowing
these eloquent words found in The Song of Songs in the
Bible. _____ (the groom), these words speak straight
from my heart:

"My beloved speaks and says to me:
'Arise, my love, my fair one, and come away:

O my dove, in the clefts of the rock,

In the covert of the cliff,

Let me see your face, let me hear your voice;

For your voice is sweet, and your face is lovely.'

My beloved is mine and I am his;

Set me as a seal upon your heart,

As a seal upon your arm;

For love is strong as death,

Passion fierce as the grave;

Its flashes are flashes of fire,

A raging flame,

Many waters cannot quench love,

Neither can floods drown it."

_____ (the groom), seal me upon your heart. To my beloved husband.

Finnish weddings have traditionally been held in midsummer because of its association with fertility, or at Christmas because it was a convenient time for a wedding—the harvest was done and there was no more work for a farmer until spring.

_____ (the groom). To our glorious future together. May it always be blessed from above by our Higher Power.

I would like to propose a toast to my husband with these words written by Ruth in the Old Testament:

"For whither thou goest, I will go,

And whither thou lodgest, I will lodge,

Thy people shall be my people,

And thy God my God.

Where thou diest, will I die,

And there I will be buried.

The Lord do so to me, and more also,

If aught but death part thee and me."

_____ (the groom), today, as I became your wife, your people became my people, your God became my God, and we will lodge together for the rest of our lives as husband and wife. I thank God for bringing you to me as part of His perfect plan. To my husband, _____ (the groom).

A Christian toast

_____ (the groom), with this toast may God, who is the best maker of a marriage, combine our hearts into one.

I would like to propose a toast to my husband. _____
(the groom), I know we both believe that our marriage has
been sanctioned by God, and I want you to know that I feel
blessed beyond measure that He brought you into my life.
To my husband.

> One of the first recorded stories of
> romantic love is that of Isaac and
> Rebekah, as recorded in the Bible: And
> she became his wife and he loved her.
> —Genesis 24:67

A toast to the bride and groom

Please stand with me as we honor _____
and _____. May your love for each
other always be a reflection of the perfect love of Christ
for His church. We wish you true peace and happiness
through Him all the days of your married life.

A Christian toast

May Christ, the Light of the World, shine at the heart of
your marriage and fill you with His joy!

A Christian toast

During a traditional Jewish wedding
ceremony, the bride is not "given away"
by the parents. Rather, the parents of the
bride and groom bring them to the
wedding canopy (the *chuppah*) to be
consecrated to each other.

I would like to propose a toast to _____ and
_____. May you be blessed with the special joy
that comes from God above and with the fruit of the Spirit,
which is love. To our happy couple.

A Christian toast

Here's a toast to our bride and groom. May your married
life be filled with health, wealth, and blessings from your
Higher Power.

They say that a daffodil or a daisy in the
bride's bouquet will ensure a sunny
marriage.

I would like to propose a toast of congratulations to our newlyweds. _____ and _____ , what an incredible wedding day this is. It is a day unlike any other: no ordinary day, this day, but a day that brings you together in God's divine providence; no ordinary flowers, these flowers, but flowers whose scents waft over us, sweet reminders of the beautiful world He has created for us; no ordinary rings, these rings, but rings that form never-ending circles, sweet reminders of your never-ending love; and finally, no ordinary vows, your vows, those promises made from your innermost hearts, sweet reminders of your never-ending commitment to each other.

To _____ and _____. May God hold you always in the hollow of His hand.

> Whatsoever God hath joined together, let no man put asunder.
> —Matthew 19:6

This is a toast to _____ and _____. May your marriage be touched by God's love, a love that's as soft as the dawn, as radiant as the sun, as bright as the morning, and as beautiful as your wedding day.

May the Source of Life bless your marriage with all that is loving and true and good. May He bless your home and your hearts each day with joy and happiness. May you share each other's joys, bear each other's burdens, and may good fortune and laughter be with you from this day on and forevermore.

Often, a homily is added to a wedding service; a homily is a short commentary or elaboration on the marriage theme.

_____ and _____ , what a beautiful couple you are—glowing with love for each other and your love for the Lord. As we raise our glasses in toast to you this hour, our prayers go with you for a marriage committed to Him, controlled by Him, and blessed by Him. One word of advice: Remember before you go to bed each night to give all your troubles to God...He's going to be up all night anyway. Seriously though, nothing could be more precious than a marriage fully committed to the will of God, and that is my wish and prayer for you today!

A Christian toast

I would like to propose a toast to our happy couple. May your marriage be guided by the hand of God; may your home be happy, contented, and filled with His Spirit; and may He bless you every day of your lives. To _____ (the bride) and _____ (the groom).

A Christian toast

To _____ and _____: May God guide you, protect you, and keep you close to Him.

A toast by the wife to her husband (or husband to wife) on their reaffirmation day or wedding anniversary

_____ (the husband or the wife), you're a very special man (or woman) and a very special husband (or wife)— loving, thoughtful, and giving. You have the kind of strength that comes from your deep faith in God and the kind of wisdom that comes from knowing God's word. The life we have shared all these years is a beautiful reflection of His love, and I thank God for you. Bless you, my husband (or wife).

A toast by the bride or groom to the parents

I would like to propose a toast to my parents. Mom and Dad, thank you for raising me in a Christian home with Christian values. Because of you I have a strong faith in God...a solid foundation for life and for marriage. No child could receive a more precious legacy than that. I love you both.

A Christian toast

The groom's family and friends usually sit on the right side of the aisle during the wedding ceremony, and the bride's on the left. This custom has developed from the age-old courtesy of seating honored guests on the right of the host. On the wedding day, the parents of the bride are considered the hosts and the parents of the groom the honored guests.

A toast by the bride to her mother

It has been said that God listens with the deepest care to a mother's prayers. I'm sure this has been true with your prayers. Thank you for being a woman of faith. Thank you for praying for me. Thank you for being my Mom. I love you.

Chapter 9

Toasts With Ethnic Variations

This chapter includes many popular wedding toasts and phrasings used around the world today. Also included is a list of the toasting beverages preferred by toasters of various nationalities and ethnic groups.

Albanian

Nga mot gëzuar.

> (Happiness for many years.)

Rrofsh sa malet.

> (May you live as long as the hills.)

Te kini shendene.

   (May you enjoy good health.)

Angolan
A sua felicidade!

   (To your happiness!)

Arabic
Hanya!

   (Good health!)

Argentinean
Salud!

   (To your health!)

The tradition of throwing rice stems from a superstition that the devil wanted everyone to be miserable, including the bride and groom. It was believed possible to "buy off" any hateful spirits by "feeding" them handfuls of rice. Some cultures merely consider rice a symbol of fertility and good luck. Today, however, rice-throwing is rarely allowed because it makes birds sick. Throw birdseed instead.

Australian
Cheers!

Austrian

Prosit!

    (May it be to your health!)

Bolivian

Salud!

    (To your health!)

Brazilian

Saude!

    (To your health!)

British

I give you a toast—May you always be two out and one in:
Out of debt, out of danger—and in good health!

All good things to you!
May your journey be good
On the road that you choose
Though it be fast or slow
And Joy attend you all the way
Whichever road you go.

                          An old Yorkshire toast

An English bride and her wedding party always walked together to the church, the procession led by a small girl who scattered blossoms along the path in front of the bride so that her life would be happy and laden with flowers.

Canadian

English: Cheerio!

(Good times!)

French: A vôtre santé and a la vôtre!

(To your health and to yours!)

Innuit Eskimo: Chimo!

(Hail!)

Chinese

Kan pei!

(Bottoms up!)

Columbian

Brindo por (the names of the bride and groom).

(I drink for [the names of the bride and groom].)

The coronation of a queen often took place at her wedding; this ritual among the nobility was soon mimicked by the commoners, who were often crowned during their wedding ceremonies as they wore ceremonial costumes resembling those of the higher class.

Dutch
Op je gezondheid!

(To your health!)

Egyptian
Al salamu alaycum!

(Peace be with you!)

Estonian
Parimat tulevikuks!

(Best for your future!)

Ethiopian
Letanachin!

(To your health!)

French
A vôtre santé, bonheur et prospérité!

(To your health, happiness, and wealth!)

Je leve mon verre a votre sante.

(I raise my glass to your health!)

Ici a la ange avec un demander pour un diable! Moi!

(Here's to an angel with a yearning for a devil! Me!)

Gaelic

Sheed Arth!

(May you enjoy the good things of life!)

Slainte mhath, slainte mhor.

(Good health, great health!)

Slaynt as shee as Aash dy vea, as Maynry's son dy Bragh.

(Health and peace and ease of life, and happiness
forever.)

During the ceremony, the German bride
and groom hold candles trimmed with
flowers and ribbons, which may be
relighted on their first wedding
anniversary.

German

Ein Prosit der Gemutlichkeit.

(A toast to easygoing, happy-go-lucky living.)

Ofen warm, Bier kalt, Weib jung, Wein alt.

(Oven warm, beer cold, wife young, wine old.)

When a couple is married in Bavaria, tradition says that the bride should arrive at the church on a hay cart; then, after the wedding, the couple saws a log in half, a ritual meant to symbolize a shared life and shared work.

Greek

Stin ygia sou!

(To your health!)

Rather than a bouquet, which symbolizes fertility, Greek-American brides throw a pomegranate.

Gypsy

May you live until a dead horse kicks you!

Haitian

A vôtre santé!

   (To your health!)

Hawaiian

Kou ola kino!

   (To your health!)

Hawaiian brides wear seven strands of pikaki flower for good luck.

Hauoli maoli oe!

   (To your happiness!)

Huapala!

   (To my sweetheart!)

During a Hindu ceremony, a gold ornament on a yellow string, known as a *thali* (gold is the traditional color of approval and good fortune), is tied around the bride's neck. She wears it throughout her marriage, its three knots reminding her of her duty to her parents, husband, and sons.

Indian (Hindu)

Aap ki sehat ke liye!

(To your health!)

Native American (Western)

Now, as you join your life together, intertwining your pasts, weaving them into one future, may the texture be especially strong, and may your pattern be especially beautiful.

Inspired by the beautiful textiles woven by the Mayan people of Highland Guatemala and Mexico

"You are my husband (or wife),

My feet shall run because of you.

My feet, dance because of you.

My heart shall beat because of you.

My eyes, see because of you.

My mind, think because of you.

And I shall love because of you."

_____(the bride or the groom), you are my reason to run, to dance, to see, to think, to live, but most of all, you are my reason to love. To my husband (or wife), _____(the bride or groom).

Inspired by an old Eskimo Indian wedding prayer

I would like to propose a toast to my bride (or bridegroom): May we each be shelter to the other; may we each be warmth to the other; and may our days be good and long upon this earth.

Inspired by an Apache Indian prayer

On their wedding morning, Hopi couples greet the rising sun and pray for a good life together, for children and for faithfulness to each other.

I would like to propose a toast to my beautiful bride: You are as fair as the white star of twilight, as clear as the sky at the end of the day, as fair as the moon's soft light. You, my precious bride, are my heart's friend.

Inspired by a traditional Shoshone Indian love poem

What is love?...It is the morning and the evening star. Thank you for loving me and becoming my wife. You are my morning and evening star.

Inspired by the traditional sayings of the
Great Plains Indians

May you walk in beauty.

Beauty before you,

Beauty behind you,

Beauty above and below you.

It is finished in beauty.

It is finished in beauty.

Inspired by the words of a Navajo song

The Sioux Indians have this expression: "With all beings and all things we shall be as relatives." _____ (the bride), as we recited our vows this morning, not only did we become related to each other as husband and wife, but we became related to each other's families. I became part of your family and you became part of mine. To my bride, _____ (the bride)—welcome to my family.

Inspired by the traditional sayings of the Sioux Indians

May you have the strength of eagle's wings,

and the faith and courage to fly to new heights,

and the wisdom of the universe to carry you there.

Inspired by a Native American blessing

Irish

May the road rise up to meet you.

May the wind be always at your back.

May the sun shine warm upon your face,

The rains fall soft on your fields.

And until we meet again, may the Lord

Hold you in the hollow of his hand.

Don't walk in front of me,

I may not follow.

Don't walk behind me,

I may not lead.

Walk beside me,

And just be my friend.

An Irish bride sews a piece of fine Irish lace into the hem of her wedding gown.

May the saints protect you,

And sorrow neglect you,

And bad luck to the one

That doesn't respect you.

May the holy Saints be about your bed, and about your
board, from this time to the latter end.

May you have warm words on a cold evening,
A full moon on a dark night.
May the roof above you never fall in,
And the friends gathered below never fall out.
May you never be in want,
And always have a soft pillow for your head.
May you be 40 years in heaven,
Before the devil knows you're dead.
May you be poor in misfortunes, rich in blessings,
Slow to make enemies and quick to make friends.
But be you rich or poor, quick or slow,
May you know nothing but happiness
from this day forward.

A combination of traditional Irish toasts

Here is to loving, to romance, to us
May we travel together through time.
We alone count as none, but together we're one,
For our partnership puts love to rhyme.

Here's to your health
May God bring you luck
And may your journey be smooth and happy.

To a full moon on a dark night
And the road downhill all the way to your door.

Here's to health, peace, and prosperity;
May the flower of love never be nipped by the frost of
disappointment.
May there always be work for your hands to do.
May your purse always hold a coin or two.
May the sun always shine on your windowpane.
May a rainbow be certain to follow each rain.
May the hand of a friend always be near you.
May God fill your hearts with gladness to cheer you.

May you look back on the past with as much pleasure as you
look forward to your future.

May the Irish hills caress you.

May her lakes and rivers bless you.

May the luck of the Irish enfold you.

May the blessings of St. Patrick behold you.

May you have many children,

And may they grow as mature in taste,

And healthy in color,

And as sought after

As the contents of this glass.

May your fire never go out.

May your well never run dry.

 Tradition says that June is a "lucky month" because of ties with Juno, Roman goddess of marriage and femininity. Also, many cultures have decided that June is the best month because it has the "luckiest weather," a sign that the bride will be happy.

Italian

Viva l'amor!

(Long live love!)

Cin-cin!

(All things good to you!)

In the Philippines, the wedding guests throw money at the feet of the bridal couple as they perform their wedding dance, called the *ado*.

Japanese

Konotabi wa omedeto gozaimasu.

(Congratulations to the bride and groom.)

"Often words cannot reflect the thousand recesses of the heart." My love for you cannot be expressed in words, but with this toast, I pass it all from my heart to yours.

"You have become for me a world of happiness and celebration...now I can imagine no other place for my heart." To my wife (or husband), _____.

Inspired by the poetry of Japan

Jewish

L'chayim!

   (To life; to your health!)

There is a Yiddish saying that goes like this: "God gave burdens, also shoulders." _____ (the bride or the groom), as we face our future together as husband and wife, may I be your shoulder to lean on, to cry on, to turn to whenever things get tough. To my wife (or husband), _____ (the bride or the groom)—may I always be there for you.

Inspired by a Yiddish saying

Mazel tov!

   (Congratulations!)

Jordanian

Besehtak!

   (To your health! Good luck! Success! Happiness!)

Korean
Chu-kha-ham-ni-da!

> (Congratulations!)

Lebanese
Sihatikom!

> (To your health!)

Lithuanian
Laimingo sugyvenimo, sviesiu dienu ir sekmingo gyvenemo abiem.

> (A happy cohabitation, sunny days, and successful life to both of you.)

Mexican
Salud y tu amor!

> (To your health and to your love!)

The godparents of a Mexican bride and groom offer a prayer book, rosary and kneeling pillow for the ceremony. After the vows, a single loop of rosary beads, symbolizing unity, is placed around the couple's neck.

Moroccan
Sahtek!

> (To your health!)

Polish

Na zdrowie, azeby nasze dzieci mialy bogatych rodzicow!

(To our health—may our children have rich parents!)

Na zdrowie i dtugie zycie!

(To your health and long life!)

Portuguese

Saúde e gôzo!

(Health and enjoyment!)

A sua felicidade!

(To your happiness!)

Romanian

Noroc!

(Good luck!)

Russian

Za Zdorovie molodech!

(To the health of the young couple!)

Russian couples are given two blessed loaves on their wedding day, one to be eaten and the other to be kept, thus ensuring a happy and prosperous marriage.

Saudi Arabian

Hanian!

(Congratulations!)

Scandinavian

Skål!

(Your health!)

The Assyrians, Hebrews, and Egyptians gave a sandal as a token of good faith when transferring property or making a deal. In fact, it became customary to throw a sandal onto a piece of land to show that the new owner was taking possession. Eventually, it became a British tradition for a father to give his new son-in-law one of the bride's shoes, signifying a transfer of authority. Today, the bride's father ties old shoes to the bumper of the getaway car as a way of saying, "She's all yours now!"

Scottish

Here's health tae yer body
An' wealth tae yer purse
An' Heav'n tae yer saul—
I wiss ye nae worse!
May the best ye've ever seen
Be the worst ye'll ever see,
May a mouse ne'er leave yer girnal
Wi a tear drap in his 'ee,
May ye aye keep hale and he'rty
Till yere auld enough tae dee,
May ye aye be juist as happy
As I wish ye aye tae be.

Spanish

Salud, pesetas y amor...y tiempo para gozarlos!
   (Health, money, and love...and time to enjoy them!)

Salud y amor sin suegra!
   (Health and love without a mother-in-law!)

Swiss

German: Gesund wohl!
French: A vôtre santé!
Italian: Salute!
   (All mean: "To your health!")

In Switzerland the junior bridesmaid leads the procession from the ceremony to the reception with a basket full of colored handkerchiefs for the wedding guests. Whoever wants one of these handkerchiefs contributes money toward the couple's first nest egg.

Thai

Chai yo!

(To your health and well-being!)

Turkish

Serefinize!

(To your honor!)

Venezuelan

A la salud!

(To your health!)

Welsh

Eiechid da, a whye fahr!

(Good health and lots of fun!)

A Welsh bride's bouquet is often laid on the grave of a parent or grandparent.

Preferred toasting beverages

Afghanistan	A nonalcoholic beverage, usually a soft drink	**Cuba**	Rum
		Denmark	Schnapps
		Ecuador	Chicha
Albania	Cognac	**Egypt**	A nonalcoholic beverage
Algeria	Coffee or tea		
Angola	Wine		
Argentina	Mate (a nonalcoholic drink)	**El Salvador**	Wine
		Finland	Vodka
		France	Champagne
Australia	Beer	**Germany**	Beer
Austria	Beer	**Great Britain**	Scotch whiskey, beer, or wine
Bahamas	Rum		
Belgium	Beer or wine		
Bermuda	Rum	**Greece**	Retsina wine
Bolivia	Rum	**Guatemala**	Aguardiente
Brazil	Cachaca	**Haiti**	Rum
Bulgaria	Plum brandy	**Honduras**	Rum
Canada	Canadian whiskeys and beers	**Iceland**	Schnapps
		India	A soft drink
		Iran	A nonalcoholic beverage
Chile	Pisco (a grape liquer) or Chilean wine		
		Iraq	Arak, coffee, or tea
China	Mao t'ai		
Columbia	Aguardiente or rum	**Ireland**	Irish whiskey
		Israel	Wine
Costa Rica	Guaro or chirrite	**Italy**	Wine

Jamaica	Rum		**Qatar**	Soft drinks or water
Japan	Sake (rice wine)		**Russia**	Vodka
Korea	Sauju (rice wine)		**Saudi Arabia**	Coffee, tea, or soft drinks
Kuwait	A nonalcoholic beverage		**Scotland**	Scotch whiskey
Mexico	Tequila or pulque		**Singapore**	Brandy
Monaco	Champagne		**South Africa**	Beer or wine
Mongolia	Vodka		**Spain**	Spanish wines or brandies
Morocco	A soft drink		**Sweden**	Akvavit (with or without a beer chaser)
Netherlands	Dutch gin			
New Zealand	Beer or wine		**Switzerland**	Eau de vie (a drink resembling kirsch)
Nicaragua	Flor de cana (a local rum)			
Nigeria	Any beverage		**Thailand**	Scotch whiskey
Norway	Aquavit		**Turkey**	Raki
Panama	Wine		**U.S.A.**	Champagne, wine, or wedding punch
Paraguay	Canna (a local brandy)			
Peru	Disco (grape-based brandy)		**Uruguay**	Grappa, cana, ron, or cognac
Philippines	Champagne, wine, or tuba (fermented palm juice)		**Venezuela**	Rum
			Wales	Beer
Poland	Polish vodka		**Zaire**	Maluvo akapia (corn liquor)
Portugal	Port wine			

Chapter 10

Toasts Inspired by the Classics

Included here are toasts inspired by classical writings, many of which are so beautifully pure they can be used without anything added, if you so desire. All quoted material incorporated into the toasts is enclosed with quotation marks.

A toast by the groom to his bride

"Come live with me and be my Love,

And we will all the pleasures prove

That hills and valleys, dales and fields,

Or woods or steepy mountain yields."

To _____ (the bride), my wife, my love.

> Inspired by the writings of Christopher Marlowe

Robert Burns has written these words: "But to see her was to love her, Love but her, and love for ever."

_____ (the bride), I fell in love with you the first time I saw you—that day at the company picnic. The skeptics say this isn't possible—love at first sight. But I know better and you do, too. To my wife,

_____ (the bride), and our forever-kind-of-love.

> A good marriage is the union of two forgivers.
> —Ruth Bell Graham (wife of Billy Graham)

"Shall I compare thee to a summer's day? Thou art more lovely and more temperate." _____
(the bride), there is nothing that can be compared to your loveliness. You're the most beautiful bride I've ever seen. And nothing can be compared to my love for you. To my wife.

Inspired by the writings of William Shakespeare

I would like to propose a toast to my bride, _____ (the bride). William Wordsworth wrote these words:

"A perfect Woman, nobly plann'd,

To warn, to comfort, and command;

And yet a Spirit still and bright

With something of angelic light."

_____ (the bride), you are my angel, my godsend, and I lift my glass in toast to you.

A successful marriage requires falling in love many times—with the same person.
—Robert Wagner

_____ (the bride), I propose this toast to you on this our wedding day. It has been said, "What greater thing is there for two human souls than to find that they are joined for life?" Our love was destined to be, and a great and marvelous thing happened here today as we joined hands, recited our vows, and became one. Here's to my wife, my soul mate for life.

Inspired by the writings of George Eliot

I would like to propose a toast to my lovely bride,
_____. Thoreau wrote these words that so beautifully
describe the way I feel today: "There is no remedy for love
but to love more." _____ (the bride), my love for you
is so deep and so intense that it engulfs my entire being and,
as Thoreau has said, the only cure for this painful malady is
to love you more, and that's exactly what I intend to do—
love you even more with each passing day. To you,
_____ (the bride).

I would like to propose a toast to my wife, _____ (the
bride). The great writer Nicholas Breton had this to say
about a wife: "A good wife is a world of wealth, where just
cause of content makes a kingdom in conceit; she is the eye
of wariness...and the heart of love; a companion of kindness,
a mistress of passion, an exercise of patience, and an
example of experience: she is the kitchen physician, the
chamber comfort, the hall's care, and the parlour's
grace...her voice is music...her mind virtuous, and her soul
gracious: she is her husband's jewel...her neighbor's love,
and her servant's honour...in sum, she is God's blessing, and
man's happiness, earth's honour and Heaven's creature."
These words, although written almost 400 years ago, could

have been said about you, _____ , for you have all of these qualities, and many more. You are indeed my jewel and God's great blessing to me. To my wife!

> All that a husband or wife really wants is to be pitied a little, praised a little, appreciated a little.
> —Oliver Goldsmith

_____ (the bride), "beauty is the gift of God," and you are indeed blessed with His gift. But your beauty runs deep, and I love not only the way you appear on the outside, but the way you *are* on the inside, where no one can see. May I be worthy of such beauty. To _____ (the bride).

Inspired by the writings of Aristotle

I would like to propose a toast to _____ (the bride). It has been said that "he loves but little who can say and count in words, how much he loves." _____ (the bride), you will never know how deeply I love you because in a lifetime of trying I will never find enough words to express how I feel. Thank you for becoming my wife. To _____ (the bride).

Inspired by the writings of Dante Alighieri

"She is mine own, and I as rich in having such a jewel, as twenty seas, if all their sands were pearl, the water nectar and the rocks pure gold." _____ (the bride), you are my jewel, my nectar, mine own. How I treasure you as my wife!

Inspired by the writings of William Shakespeare

> The sum which two married people owe to one another defies calculation. It is an infinite debt, which can only be discharged through all eternity.
> —Goethe

Victor Hugo has written that "the greatest happiness of life is the conviction that we are loved, loved for ourselves, or rather loved in spite of ourselves." _____ (the bride), thank you for loving me just the way I am. To my wife!

A toast by the bride to her groom

Elizabeth Barrett Browning said that the "earth's crammed with heaven." _____ (the groom), I am so happy to be your wife that my heart feels crammed full of heaven. Thank you for choosing me. To you, _____ (the groom).

Edith Wharton is quoted as saying, "The moment my eyes fell on him, I was content." _____ (the groom), the first time I laid eyes on you I was overcome with a sense of peace and contentment. Even at first sight, I knew you were the one. We're so right for each other! To our marriage!

The great poet Edwin Markham has written that "all that we send into the lives of others comes back into our own." _____ (the groom), the more I love you, the more love you return. I am filled to overflowing with my love for you, but I'm overwhelmed by the love you send back in return. How can such a thing be? It is a mystery. Thank you, _____ (the groom).

There is nothing nobler or more admirable than when two people who see eye to eye keep house as man and wife, confounding their enemies and delighting their friends.
—Homer

I would like to propose a toast to my husband, _____ (the groom).

> "How do I love thee? Let me count the ways.
>
> I love thee to the depth and breadth and height
>
> My soul can reach, when feeling out of sight
>
> For the ends of being and ideal grace."

Here's to a lifetime of loving you.

Inspired by the writings of Elizabeth Barrett Browning

It has been said that "the universal human yearning is for something permanent, enduring, without shadow of change." _____ (the groom), thank you for loving me with this kind of changeless love. I am assured in my heart that your love will never stumble, never falter, never fade. I am so blessed to have you for my husband. To _____ (the groom).

Inspired by the writings of Willa Cather

According to Shakespeare, "love comforteth like sunshine after rain." _____ (the groom), thank you for your love. It is indeed sunshine to my soul.

I would like to propose a toast to my husband, _____
(groom) with this poem by Anne Bradstreet:

"I prize thy love more than whole mines of gold

Or all the riches that the East doth hold.

My love is such that rivers cannot quench,

Nor aught but love from thee give recompense,

Thy love is such I can no way repay,

The heavens reward thee manifold, I pray.

Then while we live, in love let's so persevere

That when we live no more, we may live ever."

Married couples who love each other tell each other a thousand things without talking.
—Chinese proverb

A toast by the bride to her groom or by the groom to his bride, suitable for second marriages

I would like to toast my wife (or husband) with these words written by a very wise man named Socrates: "One word frees us of all the weight and pain of life: that word is love."

_____ (the bride or groom), thank you for your

love—it has melted away my pain, freed me from temporal cares and lightened my life with inexpressible joy. To my wife (or husband)!

A toast to the bride and groom

Martin Luther has said that "there is no more lovely, friendly, and charming relationship, communion, or company than a good marriage." And that is what we have here today—a really *good* marriage, the kind that will last into eternity. We all see it; we all know it. Here's to _____ and _____. May your married life be a charming relationship and a lovely communion of spirits.

Before I toast _____ and _____ , I would like to read a lovely passage about married life written by Kahlil Gibran:

> "Marriage is the union of two divinities that a third might be born on earth. It is the union of two souls in a strong love for the abolishment of separateness. It is that higher unity which fuses the separate unities within the two spirits. It is the golden ring

within a chain whose beginning is a glance, and whose ending is Eternity. It is the pure rain that falls from an unblemished sky to fructify and bless the fields of divine Nature." _____ and _____, what a beautiful thing—marriage. May your union be blessed from now to eternity. Here's to _____ and _____.

A toast by the groom to his bride on their reaffirmation day or wedding anniversary

I would like to propose a toast to my lovely bride. It has been said that "the sum which two married people owe to one another defies calculation...which can only be discharged through all eternity." How can I possibly repay you for the years of happiness you have given me? You have provided me with a haven of comfort and understanding; you have provided our children with loving guidance and nourishment; and you have provided me with countless gifts of love. I need at least another 40 years (number of years of marriage) to even begin to express my gratitude. This toast is for you, _____ (the wife). Thank you for marrying me.

Inspired by the writings of Johann Wolfgang von Goethe

Romeo said these words to Juliet: "For you and I are past our dancing days." Well, after _____ years of marriage, I can say that our dancing days have just begun. To my beautiful bride, _____ (the wife), may I have this dance for the rest of my life?

Inspired by the writings of William Shakespeare

"New love is the brightest, and long love is the greatest; but revived love is the tenderest thing known on earth."

_____ (the bride), I feel as if our love has been born anew this day—revived to its original glow and freshness. What a precious, tender thing we have here—to our love!

Inspired by the writings of Thomas Hardy

A toast by the bride to her groom on their reaffirmation day or wedding anniversary

I would like to propose a toast to my husband: "Love is the joy of the good, the wonder of the wise, the amazement of the gods." Our love has indeed been a joy and a wonder for _____ years, and just as the gods stand in amazement at

our success, so I, too, am amazed by our love. Here's to
you, _____ (the husband).

Inspired by the writings of Plato

> Only two things are necessary to keep
> one's wife happy. One is to let her think
> she is having her own way, and the other
> is to let her have it.
> —Lyndon B. Johnson

Walter Raleigh wrote these words: "But true love is a
durable fire, in the mind ever burning; never sick, never old,
never dead, from itself never turning." Our love will never
grow old—it will never die—it will burn forever.

A toast by the bride to her groom or by the groom to his bride, suitable for older couples

To my husband (or wife), _____ (the groom or the
bride). "Grow old with me! The best is yet to be, the last of
life, for which, the first is made."

Inspired by the writings of Robert Browning

My darling, we can't turn back time and be young again, but we can keep our love as young and fresh as it is today. To our love that will never grow old.

Inspired by the writings of Pierre de Ronsard

A toast to the bride by her brother or sister

_____ (the bride), I'm proud to be your brother (or sister). You're the best sister a guy (or gal) could ever have. You've always been there for me, rescuing me, advising me and, best of all, being a friend to me. Today you became _____ (the groom's) wife—what a lucky day for him!—but you will always be my sister, and I'll cherish your friendship for the rest of my life. To my sister, _____ (the bride).

Inspired by the writings of Christina Georgina Rossetti

Chapter 11

Humorous Toasts

Here are the four most popular ways to interject humor into a wedding toast:

1. The humorous anecdote.
2. The "little joke."
3. The limerick.
4. The one-liner.

My favorite is the humorous anecdote, not only because it personalizes the toast, but because it is so easy to deliver. Almost anyone can tell a little story about the bride or groom, but it takes a certain amount of timing to tell a joke, recite a limerick, or toss off a one-liner with style. Regardless of your speaking ability, however, I'm sure you will find something here you can use, even if only an idea that will trigger your own creativity. When interjecting humor into your toast, try not to offend anyone in the room, and always end the toast with a serious heartfelt sentiment.

> They say that if you lose your wedding ring, bury a dishrag, and by the time the dishrag has rotted away, you will find the ring.

The humorous anecdote

According to the dictionary, an anecdote is a "short narrative of an interesting, amusing, or biographical incident." When an anecdote precedes a wedding toast, it is usually a fascinating real-life story about the bride or groom.

There are several examples scattered throughout this book which you may want to go back and reread if you're considering telling a humorous anecdote.

Chapter 2

A family friend tells about a trip to Disneyland when the groom was a young boy and how the boy preferred watching the workers lay cement to going on the rides. (See pages 45.)

Chapter 3

The best man tells a story of how he and the groom used to scrounge around their college dorm room looking for enough loose change to get them by until the first of the month. (See page 50.)

The best man tells a story about the first time he met the groom at a company Christmas party and how the groom subtly snubbed the antics of the single women. (See page 53.)

The best man tells how he got the bride and groom together by inviting the groom to a fitness club where the bride worked. (See page 60.)

Chapter 4

The bride's father talks about what a tomboy his daughter was as she was growing up and how she's changed. (See page 69.)

Chapter 5

The groom's father tells the story of his son's sudden interest in jewelry stores and subsequent purchase of an engagement ring. (See page 74.)

The groom's father tells how the groom differs from his brothers because he always wanted to do something dangerous and adventuresome and was fortunate to find a wife who loves the same kind of thing. (See page 78.)

Chapter 12

The bride's best man tells a story of when they were kids and got lost in the dark trying to find their way home after a hike. (See page 182.)

The groom's best woman tells how the groom helped her get over an unrequited crush on an older boy when she was a skinny, pimply, stringy-haired junior high girl. (See page 183.)

Personal stories such as these are always more interesting than something canned or clichéd.

Because an anecdote must be a personal story that really happened, I can't dictate a story for you to tell. You'll need to squeeze the memories out of your own brain, I'm afraid, but hopefully there are many humorous incidents to recall. If you rack your brain and you can't think of a thing, interview the couple's parents, friends, coworkers, brothers, or sisters— there's bound to be at least one funny story you can tell without embarrassing the bride or groom.

The Guinness Book of World Records reports that the oldest recorded bridegroom was Harry Stevens, age 103, who married Thelma Lucas, age 84, at the Caravilla Retirement Home in Wisconsin on December 3, 1984.

The "little joke"

Another way to spice up your toast is to tell a little joke at the beginning of your toast, but it doesn't necessarily have to be wedding-related to work. You can include a joke about the bride's or groom's profession, their hobbies, their characteristics, how they met, where they went to college and so forth. For example, if the groom has been involved in a recent fender-bender, you could include a joke about bad drivers, or if the bride is a nurse, you could tell a joke about the medical profession, or if either likes to fish or play golf, there are hundreds of jokes from which to choose.

And where do I find these jokes, you ask? At your local library. Just ask your reference librarian to point you to the section called "humor," where you will find several shelves full of joke books. Bring a few home with you and look for jokes that can be modified to use in your toast. For example, if the groom happens to be an avid golfer, look through the table of contents for jokes about golf. Or if the bride is a teacher, look for an adaptable joke under the category of "teaching" or "campus life."

Once you've found an appropriate joke, personalize it so that it sounds like it happened to the bride or the groom. Here are a few examples that demonstrate how easily this can be done:

Courtship

You know, _____ (the bride) always hoped a handsome prince like _____ (the groom) would come riding up on horseback to rescue her from the single life. Then, sure enough, one night it happened. _____ (the groom) came riding up, climbed a vine to her bedroom window and swooped her up in his arms. They went back down the vine and onto his waiting horse. As they rode off into the moonlight, _____ (the bride) breathlessly whispered to her dashing prince, "Where are you taking me?"

"That's up to you," he said. "It's *your* dream!"

It was really strange the day _____ (the groom) called _____ (the bride) on the telephone to propose to her. He said, "_____ (the bride), I've got a little money saved up, I only have one more payment to make on my car, and I'm hoping to be able to put a down payment on a little home pretty soon. I think it's about time for me to settle down. Will you marry me?"

_____ (the bride) replied, "Of course I will, sweetie—but who is this calling?"

An English bride sometimes throws a plate full of cake crumbs from an upstairs window of her home, plate and all; the more pieces the plate breaks into, the better her luck.

Did you hear what happened when _____ (the bride) wore her engagement ring to work the first day? One of her coworkers stood admiring it and then gave her this bit of advice: "Listen, honey, whatever you do, once you're married, don't give in to him too easily. Demand your rights. Why, when I got married I made my husband promise to give up all his sinful ways."

"And did he?" asked _____ (the bride).

"I don't know," said the woman. "I haven't seen him for 10 years."

The bride

The other day one of _____ (the bride's) little neighbors asked why _____ (the bride's) wedding dress was going to be white. _____ (the bride) answered, "Well, honey, because the color 'white' stands for joy. That's why a bride wears white when she gets married—it's the most joyous day in her life."

"Then why," asked the little girl, "does the groom wear black?"

(The father of the groom rises and makes a big show of taking a glass case out of his pocket, unsnapping the case and withdrawing a pair of very dark sunglasses, which he carefully places over his eyes.)

Whew! That's better. They say a bride is supposed to be radiant, but this is ridiculous. I have to shield my eyes to look at her. Tell me...have you ever seen a more beautiful bride in your life? And, of course, they say that the groom should beam with happiness. Look at this guy...I can feel the glow all the way over here. Truthfully, though (as he removes his sunglasses), you are a beautiful couple, and Mom and I couldn't be happier for you. I toast you, _____ and _____ , and may your future be filled with the same glowing radiance and incandescent brilliance we see in you today.

The groom

_____ (the groom) writes _____ (the bride) such passionate love letters. She showed one to me the other day that read: "My dearest _____ (the bride). There is nothing I wouldn't do to be with you. I would climb the highest mountain. I would swim the deepest sea. I would cross the hottest desert. You are my beloved, and I would do absolutely anything to be near you." Then, at the end of the letter was this: "P.S. See you Saturday, if it doesn't rain."

Husbands

I overheard _____ (the bride) asking _____ (the groom) this question: "What is an average husband?"

_____ (the groom) answered: "An average husband, honey, is one who isn't quite as good as his wife thinks he is before she marries him, and not half as bad as she thinks he is afterward."

The wedding anniversary

Do you know what _____ (the wife) and _____ (the husband) did to celebrate their anniversary? They went to a romantic movie. When they got home, _____ (the wife) asked _____ (the husband), "Why don't you ever make love to me like that?" _____ (the husband) replied, "Do you know what those fellows get paid for doing that?"

The teacher (or professor)

_____ (the bride or groom) is a great teacher (or professor), but he (or she) grades tough. The other day he (or she) gave a mid-term exam and one of her (or his) students didn't know a single answer to the questions, so the student wrote across the top of the test: "God only knows."

_____ (the bride or groom) graded the test and returned it to the student with these words: "God gets an 'A'—you get an 'F.'"

The doctor

We all know that _____ (the bride or groom) is one of our town's finest surgeons, but a funny thing happened the other day in the hospital where he works. As one of the patients was being wheeled into the recovery room after surgery, he said, "Thank God that's over."

"Don't be so sure," said the patient lying next to him in the room. "They left a sponge in me and had to cut me open again to get it out."

Then another patient said, "Why they had to open me up again, too, to recover one of their instruments."

Just then _____ (the bride or groom) stuck her (or his) head in the door and called, "Anyone seen my hat?"

The lawyer

I asked _____ (the bride or groom) how he (or she) came to be such a successful lawyer. He (or she) said that it's because of some great advice he (or she) received from one of his (or her) law professors who said, "When you're in court, if the facts are on your side, hammer them at the jury; if the law is on your side, hammer that into the judge; if you have neither the facts nor the law on your side, you can still win the case—just hammer real hard on the table."

The golfer

We all know that _____ (the groom) is quite a golfer, but the other day he was having a really bad day. He was playing Pebble Beach and continually hooking his drives. By the time he reached the 18th tee box, he was seething with disgust. After another errant tee shot that hooked into Carmel Bay 50 feet below, he mumbled under his breath: "How can anyone be expected to hit a decent shot with all those darned sailboats rushing back and forth?"

The fisherman

_____ (the groom) just loves to fly-fish, and the other day he spent six hours fishing along Stenson Creek without a bite. He had promised _____ (the bride) he would bring his catch over for her to fry up for dinner, but he didn't want to admit to her that he was coming back empty-handed. So he stopped by Luca's Fresh Fish Market on the way home and purchased six beautiful golden trout, but he asked the clerk to toss them to him over the counter one at a time. The clerk asked, "What's the idea of throwing them?"

_____ (the groom) said, "Well, I've been fishing and had no luck—but I'm no liar—I want to be able to show my fiancée the fish I caught."

The farmer

One day _____ (the groom) was late for school—he was eight or nine years old at the time—and the teacher asked him why he was late. _____ (the groom) replied, "Well, I had to take the family cow to the bull."

"Couldn't your father have done it?" asked the teacher. And _____ (the groom) replied, "Well, I guess so, but I think the bull will do a better job."

See how easy it is to alter an existing joke by personalizing it with the names of the bride and groom? If you like this idea, make a quick trip to your library where you'll find dozens of books brimming with jokes that can be modified just as easily as these were.

In the olden days, the English betrothal party was called a *flouncing*, a prelude to the modern-day engagement party.

The limerick

The dictionary says that a limerick is "a light or humorous verse form of five chiefly anapestic verses of which lines one, two, and five are of three feet and lines three and four are of two feet, with a rhyme scheme of 'aabba.' "

Well, for our purposes here, let's forget all about anapestics and metrical feet. After all, you aren't turning this thing in for a grade. All you need to know about a limerick is this:

✦ A limerick has five lines.

✦ Lines one, two, and five must rhyme with each other.

✦ Lines three and four must rhyme with each other.

Now, don't be too concerned about these "rules" either, because anything close will be just fine. Here are a few of the best-known limericks ever written. Read them out loud and you'll get the hang of limerick-writing by listening to the rhythm of the phrases:

> "There was an old man of the Cape
> Who made himself garments of crepe.
> When asked, 'Do they tear?'
> He replied, 'Here and there,
> But they're perfectly splendid for shape.' "
> —Robert Louis Stevenson

> "There once were some learned M.D.'s
> Who captured some germs of disease
> And infected a train,
> Which, without causing pain,
> Allowed hundreds to catch it with ease."
> —Oliver Herford

"As a beauty I am not a star.
There are others more handsome by far.
    But my face, I don't mind it
    For I am behind it.
It's the people in front get the jar!"

—Woodrow Wilson

"There was an old man of Blackheath
Who sat on his set of false teeth.
    Said he, with a start,
    'O Lord, bless my heart!
I have bitten myself underneath!' "

—Anonymous

Quite often it is possible to convert an existing limerick into a toast by merely changing the first line from "I once knew a girl named..." to "Here's a toast to a girl named...". But, better yet, write an original limerick personalized for the bride and groom by including mention of their professions, hobbies, characteristics, how they met and so forth. Here are a few examples of personalized limericks that were composed with a particular couple in mind:

"Here's to a sweet country miss,
Met a guy introduced by her sis.
    They courted a year
    Until it was clear
A marriage would bring wedded bliss."

"Here's to a broker named Beau,
Who knew how to make money grow.
 'Til a girl he found
 Made interest compound
And off to a wedding they'd go."

"A tow truck driver named Joe,
Found business wherever he'd go.
 'Til the girl of his dreams
 Walked by in tight jeans
Now she has *him* firmly in tow."

"They met at a cute little bistro,
In foggy San Francisco.
 Until one day
 He whisked her away
To the chapel in San Luis Obispo."

There—isn't that easy? Just take a pad of paper and a pen and start fooling around with words, and you'll be surprised at the clever limerick you will compose. Have fun!

The five rules of toasting: 1. Be simple.
        2. Be yourself.
        3. Be brief.
        4. Be prepared.
        5. Be done.

The one-liner

Short little one-liners also come in handy at the beginning of the toast to liven things up and get everyone's attention. Maybe you'll find one here you can use:

To a happy marriage: the only sport in which the trapped animal has to buy the license.

A marriage involves the giving and receiving of rings: one for the bride's ring finger and one for the groom's nose.

The average husband is worth about twice what his wife thinks of him and half what his mother thinks of him.

Any married man can have his own way as long as he agrees with his wife.

Marriage is an attempt to turn a night owl into a homing pigeon.

The honeymoon is the vacation a man takes before beginning work under a new boss.

Keep your eyes wide open before marriage, half shut afterwards.
—Benjamin Franklin

A husband is an animal who, if treated fairly, yet firmly, can be trained to do almost anything.

When I said I should die a bachelor, I did not think I should live till I were married.
—Shakespeare

A wife is a person who expects her husband to be perfect and to understand why she isn't.

It doesn't really take *that* much to get married these days: two loving people, a commitment, a handsome groom, a beautiful bride, a bag of rice...and about $25,000.

One way to find out what a woman really thinks of you is to marry her.

Love: a temporary insanity curable by marriage.
—Ambrose Bierce

You know the honeymoon is over when the breathless sighs turn to gaping yawns.

Marry the man today—you can always change him tomorrow.

_____ (the bride), please place your hand on the table in front of you. Now _____ (the groom), put your hand on top of _____ (the bride's). I want everybody in the room to see the last time _____ (the groom) has the upper hand!

Here's a piece of cowboy advice: There are two ways to argue with a woman. Neither one works.

Love is like the measles; we all have to go through it.
    —Jerome Klapka Jerome

When a wife buys on credit, she is merely displaying confidence in her husband.

A married man is one who replaces the money in his wallet with a photo of his wife.

Marriage has teeth, and him bite very hot.
    —An old Jamaican proverb

Whoever said marriage is a 50/50 proposition doesn't know the half of it.

Marriage is the only war in which you sleep with the enemy.

A good wife always helps her husband with the work around the house.

It isn't easy for a husband to get back some of his take-home pay after he takes it home.

After all is said and done, it's usually the wife who has said it and the husband who has done it.

What is a husband? A husband is that mysterious creature who buys his football tickets in June and his wife's Christmas present on December 24th.

What is a marriage? It is an alliance of two people, one who never remembers birthdays and the other who never *forgets* them.

Every young man knows when the right girl comes along because she tells him.

Men are either born with consciences or marry them.

I pray thee have me excused, I have married a wife, and therefore I cannot come.
    —Luke 14:20

Chapter 12

Special Toasts

Here is a collection of toasts that have been personalized to express those deep and tender feelings that may exist within a special relationship or in a special situation, including the following:

- ✦ A toast to the bride by her mother.

- ✦ A toast to the bride by her best friend or honor attendant.

- ✦ A toast to the bride by her best man, if the bride has chosen to have a best man instead of a maid/ matron of honor.

- ✦ A toast to the groom by his best woman, if the groom has chosen to have a best woman instead of a best man.

- ✦ A toast to the bride and groom, suitable for a second marriage.

✦ A toast by the bride to her groom or by the groom to his bride, suitable for a second marriage.

✦ A toast to the bride and groom and to the children from a previous marriage.

✦ A toast from the bride or groom to their parents.

✦ A toast from the bride or groom to their in-laws.

✦ A toast from the bride or groom to their children.

✦ A toast by the children of the bride and groom.

✦ A toast by the groom to his bride, suitable for an older couple.

✦ A toast by the bride to her groom, suitable for an older couple.

✦ A toast to the bride and groom, suitable for a second marriage.

✦ A toast to the bride and groom on their reaffirmation day or wedding anniversary.

✦ A toast in memory of a loved one.

 They say that if you cry on your wedding day, you'll have a long marriage.

A toast to the bride by her mother

One day you wake up and realize that you've given birth to your best friend. _____(the bride), you truly are my best friend, and my heart is overflowing with my love for you, my precious daughter, on this, the happiest day of your life. I have so much I'd like to say, but mere words are inadequate to express my feelings. As I helped you dress this morning—and what a beautiful bride you are—and helped arrange the veil around your sweet face, I realized that you're not a little girl anymore, but a thoughtful, caring woman with very special dreams and so much love to give to _____ (the groom). I toast you _____ (the bride), my cherished daughter and my best friend.

> The bride usually stands on the groom's left during the ceremony; this tradition goes back to the old "marriage by capture" idea where the groom needed his sword hand free for defense.

A toast to the bride by her best friend or honor attendant

I would like to propose a toast to _____ (the bride). You are the most loving, understanding friend anyone could have. No one cares from the heart like you care, and no one listens from the heart like you do. Thank you for being my "sister of the soul." I wish you a beautiful life with _____ (the groom). To my best friend, _____ (the bride).

A toast to the bride by her best man, if the bride has chosen to have a best man instead of a maid/matron of honor

_____ (the bride), the first thing I would like to say is that it is an honor for me to have been chosen as your best man. Thank you. Of course, we have been friends since we were kids, and we've been through a lot together. I remember the time—we were eight or nine years old, I think—we thought the coolest thing in the world would be to pack up our day packs with snacks and hike to the top of Tyler's Peak. Well, it took us a lot longer than we thought, and, by the time we finally got to the top, not only had we eaten all our snacks, but it was starting to get dark. Then, by the time we made it halfway back down the mountain, we were good and lost, and everyone in Tylerville came looking for us—our parents, Barton County Search and Rescue, the fire department, the police. It was your Dad who finally found us—you were sitting on that big rock crying your eyes out, and I was so scared I was shaking. At least we had our "15 minutes of fame"—we made the headlines in our little local paper the next day, the first and last time that's ever happened.

You've been a great friend to me, _____ (the bride), and it makes me happy to see you so happy.

You're a beautiful bride, just like I always knew you would be, and _____ (the groom's) a lucky guy. God bless you, as you take him by the hand and begin your new life as his wife. To you, _____ (the bride).

It was traditionally believed that evil spirits lurked around the threshold; therefore, the brave groom carried his bride through this dangerous doorway to safety and happiness on the other side. This tradition has followed us into modern-day America, with the groom still carrying his bride over the threshold of their home.

A toast to the groom by his best woman, if the groom has chosen to have a best woman instead of a best man

I would like to propose a toast to _____ (the groom). It's pretty rare these days for a woman to be asked to stand up for the groom, and I'm honored to have been asked. Because we're first cousins, we've spent a lot of time together through the years, and, in a way, I guess you could say we're as close as any brother and sister could be.

Whenever I had a problem, I could always count on you to listen. And you always had such great advice, too. Do you remember when we were in junior high and I had the big "crush" on Jim Harlowe? Of course, he was three years older and didn't even know I existed, but I would mope around and cry because he wouldn't "love me back." But you were just great—do you remember what you did? First of all, you sat me down and explained that sometimes a guy just didn't pay attention to a girl the way he should—if only he really knew what a terrific girl she was—and that he was pretty stupid if he didn't pay any attention to me. And then, trying to make me feel better, you asked me if I wanted to go with you and Carol to Marriott's to ride the bumper cars that afternoon. Looking back on it now, you could have said, "Darlene, why on earth would a good-looking guy like Jim Harlowe pay any attention to a skinny, pimply, stringy-haired girl like you? Just forget about him." But no, even though you knew that was the truth, you said just the right thing to make me feel better. Thanks for being there for me—always. You are my best friend. _____ (the bride), you're a pretty lucky gal to snag such an awesome guy.

Here's to both of you!

A toast to the bride and groom, suitable for a second marriage

I would like to propose a toast to our newlyweds. This day is especially precious because you are so blessed to be given a second chance at happiness. What a wonderful day of renewed hope and joy. It is a day of peace and contentment—a sweet calm after a cold, fearsome storm. I can speak for everyone in this room when I say that we wish you all the happiness you deserve. We are so glad you found each other, and, just remember, the best is yet to come. Here's to _____ and _____.

A toast by the bride to her groom or by the groom to his bride, suitable for a second marriage

Today I have married my best friend, my lifesaver, my healer, my sweetheart. Before I met you, _____ (the bride or groom), I was only half a person, a broken man (or woman). But your love has fallen softly on my heart and made me whole again. You are the most compassionate, tender, caring person I've ever known.

To our future!

It is a Filipino wedding tradition to serve roast pig at the reception because the pig is considered to be a symbol of fertility and prosperity.

A toast to the bride and groom and to the children from a previous marriage

I would like to propose a toast to _____ (the bride) and _____ (the groom) and _____ (a child) and _____ (a child). What a beautiful picture you make as you stand together as a new little family. I speak for everyone in this room when I tell you how happy we are for *all* of you, and we wish you all the happiness you deserve. God bless you, and go with our congratulations and best wishes for a wonderful future. Here's to you all.

A toast by the bride and groom to their parents

I would like to propose a toast to my Mom and Dad. Thank you for being such positive role models in my life. I'm proud to be your son (daughter). You have taught me how to love, to care, and to give. You were always there for me through the years, and I love you for that. Thanks, too, for all the help you've been to _____ (bride/groom) and me planning this wedding. Don't think you're getting rid of me, by the way. I plan to be back for Mom's cherry pie (or Dad's homemade ice cream, and so on.) So, save

_____ (bride/groom) and me a place at the table. We both love you so much.

> Marriage should be a duet—when one sings, the other claps.
> —Joe Murray

A toast by the bride and groom to their in-laws

I would like to propose a toast to _____'s Mom and Dad. Thank you for raising such an incredible man/ woman. I love him/her dearly, and I feel blessed to become part of your family. I hoped to find someone like

_____ (bride/groom), but I had high ideals, so I wasn't sure someone like _____ (bride/groom) even existed. Then, that day at (the association picnic, Fourth of July concert, and so on.) I met him/her and I was totally blown away. He/she did exist after all. Thank you for all the help you've given us planning this wedding. We love you both so much.

A toast from the bride or groom to their children

I would like to propose a toast to my beautiful daughter, _____. You look so pretty today, and I'm so proud to be your father/mother. Thank you for being so loving and sweet, and for welcoming _____ (the new husband/wife) into our family. We're going to have fun times together. I love you!

To my handsome son, _____. Thank you for standing beside me today as my best man. I'm so proud of you and thankful to you for loving _____ (the new husband/wife) and welcoming him/her into our family. To _____. I love you.

In Orthodox Jewish custom, the bride, escorted by the two mothers carrying lighted candles, circles the groom under the canopy before she takes her place at his right. This custom, although impressive and moving, is being observed by fewer brides in this modern day. Most rabbis, however, will add it to a wedding ceremony if asked.

A toast by the children of the bride and groom

From a young child: "To my Mommy. Thank you for getting me a new Daddy. I love you."

From an older child: "To Mom/Dad and _____ (the new step parent). Your wedding was so beautiful. Thank you asking me to be your maid of honor/best man. I love you both."

A toast by the groom to his bride, suitable for an older couple

There is an old proverb that says: "An old man in love is like a flower in winter." _____ (bride), you have made me feel like a flower in winter. Thank you for marrying me.

A toast by the bride to her groom, suitable for an older couple

It has been said that there is no surprise as magical as finding your life's mate late in life. To love and to be loved by you is like God's finger on my shoulder—an absolute miracle. To my dear husband, _____ (the groom).

A toast to the bride and groom, suitable for an older couple

I would like to propose a toast to _____ and _____. Sir Arthur Wing Pinero wrote these words:

"Those who love deeply never grow old; they may die of old age, but they die young." May your love stay forever young.

A new practice has been introduced in which the bride is escorted halfway down the aisle by her father, where they stop and are met by the groom, who comes forward, takes his bride and walks with her to the marriage altar.

A toast to the bride and groom, suitable for a second marriage.

I would like to propose a toast to _____ and _____. Today is your special day—a day of new beginnings. A day of hope for a future filled with excitement and joy. I'm so glad you found each other. Will everyone please raise their glasses and join me in this heartfelt toast to _____ and _____.

_____ and _____, I can speak for everyone here when I say that we're overjoyed you found each other, and we're happy you decided to marry. You each had bruised hearts that needed healing, and you found healing balm in each other's love and compassion. To your future—a life filled with joy, peace, and laughter.

A toast to the bride and groom on their reaffirmation day or wedding anniversary

Life is better when it's shared by two. Your trials, triumphs, laughter, hopes, and tears all helped to move you toward each other as you experienced them together. After _____ (number of years of marriage) years of married life, you have become each other's dearest friend. Here's to another _____ years of sharing and loving.

During medieval times, the Athenians made wedding-day offerings to Zeus, who was said to disapprove of the idea of marriage. To protect the bride from this god's displeasure, she was whisked away at nightfall and seated between her husband and his best man. As they made their way through the village, they were greeted and joined by friends who sang and carried torches. This became known as the bride's processional.

I would like to propose a toast to _____ and _____. Our hearts were touched today as we witnessed your renewal of your wedding vows. You've been married for ____ years, and through those years, those of us who have known you, have been impressed by your love. As you vowed to each other all those years ago, your love has carried you through good times and bad. Through sickness and health. Through times of plenty and times when things weren't quite so great. But through it all, your love has overcome adversities, and your love has rejoiced in the good times as well. Here's to another _____ years of love and joy.

We're here to celebrate 50 years of wedded bliss—it has been bliss, hasn't it? (glancing at the couple) You've been role models for the rest of us— the way your love sustained you through the good times and the bad. We've seen you dry each other's tears and applaud each other's accomplishments. You've been quite a team! Your love has touched us all. Here's to your love.

A toast by a husband to his wife on their reaffirmation day or wedding anniversary

The greatest gift I've ever received is the gift of your love. Because of your love, I feel rich. My treasure chest is overflowing with the wealth of your caring and your love. I'm proud to be your husband, and I toast you, my beloved wife.

Many Islamic brides wear red, the color of blood, signifying life.

A toast by a wife to her husband on their reaffirmation day or wedding anniversary

I would like to propose a toast to my husband. Our marriage has been a perfect blend of friendship and love. You've always been there for me, _____ (the husband), whether I needed a hug or a caress, or just someone to listen to me when I was worried or down about something. But you know what I love best about being married to you? The best part is when I wake up in the middle of the night, and I can wrap up with your loving arms around me and feel safe because you're there to hold me tight. I'm so glad I married you, and I'm proud that you've chosen to reaffirm the vows we made on that day _____ years ago. To my precious husband.

A toast in memory of a loved one

Please raise your glasses in a memorial toast to _____ (Judy's grandma, Jim's Uncle Howard, Sandy's Mom, and so on.) We know he/she would have loved to be here to see (daughter, son, niece, nephew) be married to _____. But we know he/she is here in spirit. Wouldn't he/she have loved to see _____ walk down the aisle—what a beautiful bride (or see _____ — what a handsome groom, and so on). We miss him/her and we toast him/her now in memory of his/her life and positive influence on all our lives. To _____.

The Romans believed that demonic spirits were jealous of people's happiness, so they felt that the bride would throw the devil off track by wearing a veil. The veil was also a custom in Far Eastern countries as protection from the "Evil Eye." Then, during the Crusades, the veil acquired another purpose: The bride was sold by her father, who insisted she wear a thick covering over her face so the groom wouldn't see her until after the ceremony. Then it would be too late to say, "Oh, no!" Since that time, however, the wedding veil has become a symbol of chastity and modesty.

Chapter 13

Theme Wedding Toasts

The 21st century has brought us an array of theme weddings, which require special wedding toasts appropriate to each theme.

First, we have holiday weddings, such as Valentine's Day and Christmas. Then there are nature weddings that take place outdoors, whether in a garden or along the seashore. Finally, we have the period weddings, which have gained in popularity over the past decade, such as a Renaissance or Victorian theme.

Holiday weddings

Couples often plan their weddings on a holiday, such as Valentine's Day, or during traditional family holiday get-togethers, when it's easy to assemble the family.

Following are wedding toasts for a holiday wedding.

New Year's Day (or Eve) wedding

Here's a toast to _____ and _____. I think this is pretty special—getting married on New Year's Day (or Eve)—a time for new beginnings. Bless you as you begin your lives together as husband and wife, and may all your troubles last as long as my New Year's resolutions.

I would like to wish our newlyweds well with a traditional Irish New Year's toast: May the Lord keep you in his hand and never close his fist too tight on yours. May the face of every good news and the back of every bad news be toward you in the new year.

> June is considered to be a lucky month, promising a life of sunshine, romance, and prosperity.

Valentine's Day wedding

_____ and _____ , what a good idea to be married on Valentine's Day—that way you'll never forget your wedding anniversary. Seriously, though, it is fitting to be married on such a day as this, a day set aside for couples in love. To a lifetime of love and happy Valentine's Days!

We were all touched today as you recited your marriage vows. What a perfect day to pledge your love to each other!

Valentine's Day—a day devoted to lovers and the giving of hearts in love. We toast you _____ and _____, and may your hearts always provide shelter for each other.

Christmas Day (or Eve) wedding

_____ and _____, what a lovely day (or evening) to get married, a day (or evening) poignant with the joys of giving and of love as you have given yourselves to each other in the spirit of Christmas. To a future filled with the same love and joy you feel this day (or eve).

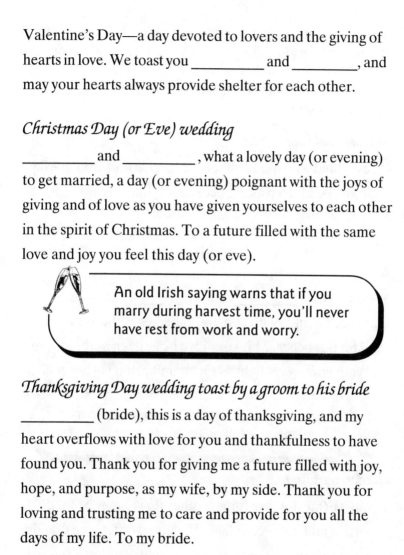

An old Irish saying warns that if you marry during harvest time, you'll never have rest from work and worry.

Thanksgiving Day wedding toast by a groom to his bride

_____ (bride), this is a day of thanksgiving, and my heart overflows with love for you and thankfulness to have found you. Thank you for giving me a future filled with joy, hope, and purpose, as my wife, by my side. Thank you for loving and trusting me to care and provide for you all the days of my life. To my bride.

Nature weddings

Outdoor weddings have become quite popular for couples who want to escape the confines of a church or any other manmade structure. An outdoor wedding evokes a natural ambience, glorious and sacred as the bride and groom are married in "God's cathedral."

Following are several toasts that are appropriate for nature weddings.

Seaside wedding

Please stand with me as we toast the bride and groom: May your joys be as deep as the ocean and your sorrows as light as its foam.

We toast you _____ and _____ . May your marriage be filled with as many blessings as the grains of sand on this beach. May your love be as deep as this ocean and your sorrows as light as the foam washing at our feet.

They say it's lucky to marry when the moon is full or waxing.

Garden wedding

I hold a beautiful rose [or any other flower may be used]. It is perfect and unique. In fact, there is no other rose exactly like it anywhere on earth. _____ and _____ , this rose symbolizes the love you have for each other—which is also beautiful and perfect in every way. May each day of your lives be as lovely as this flower. To _____ and _____ .

May your love crowd out the weeds of life, and may your marriage always be as glorious as this garden, filled with joy and beauty.

It is said that Divine love is a sacred flower, as exquisite and perfect as this tulip [or other flower] I hold in my hand, which in its early bud is happiness, and in its full bloom is heaven. May your life together be as perfect as this flower.

Adapted from a poem by Eleanora Louisa Hervey

Forest wedding

We wish you a blessed life together, as fragrant as this forest, as glorious as this sunset, and as tender as a summer shower. May your marriage be filled with sunshine, joy, and laughter. To _____ and _____.

Don't overanalyze your marriage: It's like yanking up a fragile indoor plant every twenty minutes to see how its roots are growing.
—*The Bill Balance Hip Handbook*

I toast you, _____ and _____, with an ancient Apache wedding blessing: "Now you will feel no rain, for each of you will be shelter for the other. Now you will feel no cold, for each of you will be warmth for the other. Now there is no more loneliness; now you are two persons, but there is only one life before you. Go now to your dwelling— to enter into the days of your life together—and may your days together be good and long upon the earth."

_____ and _____, we raise our glasses to you in a wedding toast. As we stand in the shade of these glorious trees, we wish you their strength. As a tree grows deeper, stronger, and grander with each year of its life, so may your marriage become. And as a tree raises its arms, reaching for strength from above, may your arms reach for each other, absorbing each others' strength.

When the bride tosses her bouquet at the end of the reception, she probably doesn't realize that the origin of this tradition is a Roman custom in which the bride kindled the hearth in her new home with a marriage torch that was hurtled among the guests.

Waterside wedding

Percy Shelley wrote a beautiful poem that fits this moment: "The fountains mingle with the river, and the rivers with the ocean. The winds of heaven mix forever with a sweet emotion; nothing in the world is single, all things by a law divine, in one spirit meet and mingle, why not I with thine?" Indeed we have witnessed today as _____ and _____ who have not only met and mingled, but joined together as husband and wife. We toast you today and wish you a lifetime of sweet heaven together.

Outdoor winter wedding

_____ and _____, we're so blessed to be here with you today to celebrate your marriage. What an idyllic setting this is, with the diamonds sparkling in the snow, the aspen quaking in the breeze, and the sun casting a glow over all. May your marriage be as glorious as this setting, filled with love and beauty for all the years to come. To _____ and _____.

Outdoor summer wedding

Please stand as we propose a toast to _____ and _____. May your married life together always be as resplendent and idyllic as this place. May your love glow as brightly as the sun shining overhead. May your troubles be as fleeting as the wispy clouds drifting toward the horizon. To _____ and _____.

Destination wedding

I speak for everyone here when I say that we would go to the ends of the earth to attend your wedding—and it seems we have done exactly that! However, even with the lost luggage, the lousy airline meals, and jet lag, we're all glad we came. Our wish is that your marriage will always be as warm, and happy and glorious as this place. To _____ and _____.

Russian and German brides wear pieces of palm in their shoes the night before the wedding, ensuring a lucky marriage.

Period weddings

Although period weddings have been popular for the past 15 years, the 21st century has brought even greater interest in Celtic, Renaissance, and Victorian weddings. This fervor has been spurred by the touching Celtic vows in the movie *Braveheart*, as well as the burgeoning popularity of Renaissance festivals.

Following are appropriate toasts for period weddings.

Celtic wedding

I would like to propose a traditional Celtic wedding toast:

_____ and _____, " may joy and peace surround you both, and may contentment latch your door. May happiness be with you now and God bless you evermore."

Author unknown

Toast for any handfasting ceremony

We have witnessed your vows and your willingness to be bound together in marriage, symbolized by your poignant handfasting ceremony. We are all touched by your commitment and we, likewise, commit ourselves to you— to be there for you, to support you, and to encourage you as you venture out as a newly wedded couple. May you be filled with joy and unity throughout your marriage life. To _____ and _____.

Victorian wedding (toast by the groom to his bride)

I would like to propose a toast to my lovely wife, with the words of Robert Burns: "O my Luve's like a red, red rose, that's newly sprung in June; O my Luve's like the melodie that's sweetly played in tune, as fair as thou, my bonnie lass, so deep in luve am I, and I will luve thee still, my dear, Till a' the seas gang dry." I love you _____ (bride). [The groom lifts his glass in toast to his bride.]

The bride traditionally wears "something old, something new, something borrowed and something blue." This custom stems from an Old English rhyme. The color blue, however, has several meanings: In ancient Israel, brides wore a blue ribbon that denoted modesty, fidelity, and love; Catholic brides wear blue to represent the purity and innocence of the Virgin Mary.

Renaissance wedding

Please raise your glasses as we toast our lovely lady and handsome knight with the words of Sir Walter Scott:

"To every lovely lady bright,

I wish a gallant faithful knight;

To every faithful lover, too,

I wish a trusting lady true."

May our lady and knight enjoy a lifetime of happiness.

My goode lords and ladies of this assembly, I pray attend ye raise high your glasses in toast to his lordship and his fairest lady wife. May we drink to their health, wealth, and abundance of joy. May their days be long and lack in sorrow. To Lord and Lady _____.

A wedding couple in Bermuda tops their wedding cake with a tiny tree sapling, which is planted in their yard when they return from their honeymoon. As the tree grows and becomes stronger each day, so does their marriage.

Chapter 14

Original Wedding Toasts

One of the greatest rewards of writing self-help books such as this one is the positive feedback I receive from my readers, especially when they send me copies of the toasts they composed with the help of my book.

I have selected excerpts from several of these letters, which I hope you'll enjoy reading as much as I have.

> This is hard to believe, but true: An original marriage custom was for a warrior to choose a certain desirable woman to be his wife. Then, with the help of a strong fellow warrior, he would capture his bride and carry her off to where the marriage would be consummated by force. This fellow warrior became known as the groom's "best man."

A toast by the groom's father and best man

This is a letter I received from the groom's father. It touched my heart because it conveyed how much this father loves his son, and felt humbled and honored to be asked to be his best man.

The father wrote: "I purchased your very fine book, titled *Complete Book of Wedding Toasts*. My son was getting married, and I was the father of the groom, and my wonderful son asked me to be his best man. What an honor!

"Because of the unique situation, I enclose a copy of my toast and thought you may want to consider it for your next printing."

> Marriage may restrict your activity, but it increases your pleasure.
> —Rev. Robert Schuller

The toast:

"When Darren asked me to be his best man, I had many emotions running through me. I was thrilled and excited, but mainly I was honored to be asked to be his best man, and very proud to be his father.

"Darren has always made his family proud. He sets his goals and through shear determination, he reaches his goals. He has dreams, and makes his dreams become a reality. What better dream could Darren have than marrying his lovely bride? And here we are, living the reality. She is a special young lady—beautiful, bright, warm, witty, kind, and all good things wrapped into one.

"Together they make the perfect couple. In fact, the more I see them together, the more I think to myself: 'These two just have to be married.'

"So, let's raise our glasses and toast our newlyweds. We wish you health, happiness, love, and friendship, and may all your wonderful dreams become reality."

Submitted by Jeffrey Fogel, Rydal, Pennsylvania.

The idea of the bride's trousseau dates back to when the bride came to her husband well-provided for (to compensate him for the big expense he was taking on by marrying her). The trousseau, which literally means "little bundle," included money or land, clothing, and goods for housekeeping. Today, a bride's trousseau is usually composed of special pieces of clothing she has purchased to wear on her honeymoon and during the first year of marriage.

A Valentine's wedding toast by the best man

I also received this beautiful letter and toast from a best man. He writes: "The bride and groom are 62 and 65 years old, respectively. Each lost a spouse to cancer three years ago. Thanks for your help (your book) with the toast. As you can see, I used phrases from your book throughout. The 130 guests loved the toast, as did the bride and groom."

The toast:

"Good evening, Monsignor, Carole, Len, family, and friends of Carole and Len.

"What a wonderful, happy occasion this is, and how appropriate—Valentine's weekend, a time set aside for couples in love.

"I was honored to be asked by Len to be his best man—most of you know me. I am Frank Cox, a friend of Len's for some 48 years. We met at Georgetown and were roommates in our sophomore, junior, and senior years (Carole, there are some things you should know—we must talk.)

"We all know who gets credit for introducing Carole and Len. . . Mary and I take primary credit for bringing Len to Larchmont from New Jersey— our families have literally grown up together, celebrating births, baptisms, confirmations, and weddings. We spent summer vacations on Long Island, winter ski trips to Vermont, apple picking in the fall, and, of course, many fun parties together.

"Len has many attributes. He's tall, handsome, smart, honest, and he has great integrity. He's generous, fair, humorous, and is a loving, compassionate person. (Len, I can't read the rest of your notes.)

"While I only first met Carole some 14 months ago, it was immediately obvious that, along with her stunning beauty, came a charming personality, a great sense of humor, intelligence, and sophistication. I feel as though we have known her for years—and everyone can see that you two are just so right for each other.

Some have said that a bride should wear three rings on her wedding day: one on her finger, a wreath on her head and a circular brooch over her heart.

"Since Carole entered into Len's life, those of us who spend a good bit of time with him, especially on the golf course—where he tends to express his true feelings— noticed he became more patient, less irritable, and less self-critical. He began to show a certain warmness, and there was a glow about him, that can only be attributed to the love you two share. (Carole, we thank you for that transformation.)

"I'm amazed, as I'm sure many of you are, at the number of values, interests, and priorities Carole and Len have in common. Would you believe they both play golf, tennis, paddle tennis, and love to dance? And they both love to watch football (how unusual is that?) and Len hopes to introduce Carole to bowling. (Good luck, Len.) They also have a common interest in fine food and fine wines.

"The marriage of Carole and Len was certainly made in heaven. Please join me in a toast—Carole and Len, we wish you a long lifetime of love and health with family and friends, and an eternity of happiness. God bless you."

When the Orthodox Jewish bridegroom crushes a glass under his foot at the end of the wedding ceremony, he metaphorically enacts his union with his bride and recalls the destruction of the Jewish Temple in Jerusalem.

A wedding toast by the bride's maternal grandfather

Richard Senter, the bride's grandfather, wrote me a lovely handwritten letter, explaining how he wrote his toast. Here are excerpts from his letter:

"Dear Mrs. Warner,

Thank you! I benefited greatly from your *Complete Book of Wedding Toasts*, especially the first chapter of instruction.

"In appreciation for the help I received, I am enclosing a copy of my toast to the bridal couple. I designed the toast to give everyone some background information, as well as anecdotes of their romance."

[He went on to explain how the wedding took place on a beach at Lake Michigan, and that the bride's and groom's families were not acquainted with each other before the wedding.]

Excerpts from his toast:

"Ladies and gentlemen, I would like to propose a toast to the newly-minted couple, Mr. and Mrs. Andrew Strahs.

"…But first, I sense a question in the air. I sense the question so strong, because so many of you are asking it. How did two newcomers to Chicago meet and decide to become one? Let me take you on a journey, and we will trace their footprints.

"It all began with Archimedes, the Greek genius who lived between 200 and 300 B.C. and did monumental work in mathematics, physics, and mechanics.

"Andrew, who was at the University of Chicago in a Ph.D. program, wanted to expand his circle of acquaintances beyond his classmates, so he became a docent at the Field Museum.

An English bride is considered lucky if she has been kissed by a chimney sweep.

"Colleen was a technical writer for a software company, and also wanted to expand her circle of acquaintances, so she also became a docent at the Field Museum.

"The Museum was preparing a special exhibit of Archimedes and his nine treatises. When the call went out for docents to handle these exhibits, by coincidence, Colleen and Andrew both volunteered.

"At the opening of the exhibit, they were both there. Andrew spotted this tiny package of perfection with the bright red hair. He talked to her, and there was a mutual attraction. Unconsciously, they started on the road so many of us have traveled—the road to romance.

"As they dated and got to know each other, the romance continued. (Now, a romance is similar to a sausage—it's better if you don't know all the ingredients!)

"…I am old. I am full of years. I am also full of memories. I know true love when I see it…

"Ladies and gentlemen, will you rise and join me in a toast to Colleen and Andrew, may your honeymoon last throughout eternity."

Grandpa Dick, Leland Michigan

The origin of having bridesmaids and groomsmen stems from an ancient belief that in order to prevent the devil from harming the bride and groom, the couple should be continually surrounded by friends who were dressed alike. It was thought that the devil would become so confused that he'd leave.

Epilogue

I hope that one of the toasts included in this book turned out to be exactly what you were hoping to find. If not, it is easy to compose your own toast, incorporating a few of your favorite phrasings and your own heartfelt sentiments about the person you will be toasting. Here are questions to ask yourself to help you create a good wedding toast:

✦ What is my relationship to the person I will be toasting?

✦ What feelings would I like to express?

✦ Which words and phrasings best express these feelings?

In conclusion, I toast you, my reader! May your toast be personal, warm, and heartfelt.

I will be updating this book from time to time, and I would appreciate receiving a copy of your wedding toasts, if you would agree to share them with me. Please send them to me in care of my publisher:

Diane Warner

c/o Career Press

P.O. Box 687

Franklin Lakes, NJ 07417.

Bibliography

Andrews, Robert. *Famous Lines: The Columbia Dictionary of Familiar Quotations*. New York: Columbia University Press, 1997.

Brown, H. Jackson, Jr. *Life's Little Treasure Book On Love*. Nashville, Tenn.: Rutledge Hill Press, 1995.

Cotner, June. *Wedding Blessings*. New York: Broadway Books, 2003.

Crockett, Laura. *The Booke of Betrothal*. New York: Dover Publications, 2000.

Grace, James. *The Best Man's Handbook*. Jackson, Tenn.: Running Press, 1999.

Jones, Leslie. *Happy Is the Bride the Sun Shines On*. New York: Contemporary Books, 1995.

Linfield, Jordan and Joseph Krevisky. *Words of Love*. New York: Random House, 1997.

Kingma, Daphne Rose. *Weddings from the Heart*. Boston, Mass.: Conari Press, 1995.

Matthews, Bette. *Wedding Toasts and Vows*. Michael New York: Friedman Publishing Company, 2001.

Naylor, Sharon. *Your Special Wedding Toasts*. Naperville, Ill.: Sourcebooks, Inc, 2004.

Noel, Darren. *Perfect Guide to Wedding Speeches and Toasts*. Canton, Ohio: PRC Publishing, 2003.

Paris, Wendy. *Words for the Wedding*. Berkley, Calif: Berkley Publishing, 2001.

Schwartz, Ronald. *The 501 Best and Worst Things Ever Said About Marriage*. New York: Citadel Press, 1995.

Steward, Arlene Hamilton. *A Bride's Book of Wedding Traditions*. New York: Hearst Books, 1995.

Washington, Peter. *Love Poems*. New York: Alfred A. Knopf, 1995.

Wogan, Barry. *Wedding Speeches and Jokes*. Berkshire, UK: Foulsham and Co., 1990.

Young, Katherine. *The Little Giant Encyclopedia of Wedding Toasts*. New York: Sterling Publishing, 2000.

Index

Also by Diane Warner

Published by John Wiley Publishing:
Single Parenting for Dummies, co-authored with Marion Peterson

Published by F & W Publications, Betterway Books:
How to Have a Big Wedding on a Small Budget, 4th edition
Big Wedding on a Small Budget Planner and Organizer
How to Have a Fabulous, Romantic Honeymoon on a Budget
Beautiful Wedding Decorations and Gifts on a Small Budget
Picture-Perfect, Worry Free Weddings
How to Have a Great Retirement on a Limited Budget

Published by Career Press/New Page Books:
Contemporary Guide to Wedding Etiquette
Best Wedding Ever

Complete Book of Wedding Vows, 2nd edition

Complete Book of Wedding Showers

Complete Book of Baby Showers

Diane Warner's Wedding Question & Answer Book

Diane Warner's Big Book of Parties

Diane Warner's Complete Book of Children's Parties

Diane Warner's Great Parties on Small Budgets

Published by Pentan Overseas, Inc. (Books on Tape)

The Perfect Wedding Planner

Published by JISTWorks, Inc. (co-authored with her husband, Jack, and Clyde Bryan):

The Unauthorized Teacher's Survival Guide, 3rd Edition

The Inside Secrets of Finding a Teaching Job, 3rd Edition

Published by Accent Books, David C. Cook Publishing:

Puppets Help Teach

Puppet Scripts for Busy Teachers